Scan to view the Savannah Shadows trailer
and get updates on new projects

SAVANNAH SHADOWS

TALES *from the* MIDNIGHT ZOMBIE TOUR

TOBIAS MᶜGRIFF

Photography by Beau Kester

Book design by Rebecca Lysen

CONTENTS

PREFACE ✦

Thankfully, most people who take a Blue Orb tour want more. The bad news, city guidelines mandate only 30 people are allowed on any one tour and most days we are forced to turn away more people than we tour.

Even with those I am fortunate to meet and guide, there just isn't enough time to cover all of the material I have or satiate the interest that exists about Savannah.

At first, I tried to tell the rest of the story through a radio show we started called *Savannah Paranormal*. It debuted on WTKS 1290, airing just before *Coast to Coast* on Saturday nights. Within a few months, we were on iTunes and had over 25,000 subscribers.

Even with the podcast (now called *Savannah Shadows*), I quickly learned I was still limited. I toyed with the idea of doing campfire type broadcasts, telling a story directly from the route. It was well received but people that listen to podcasts want a variety of guests. I wanted a variety of guests...and we were limited to 48 minutes after commercials, and only once a week.

Over time, the show started producing its own interesting stories and evocative conversations. We interviewed Father Gary Thomas, a Vatican trained exorcist who was the inspiration and consultant for *The Rite* with Anthony Hopkins. We spoke with Christopher Lutz, a child survivor of *The Amityville Horror*. We interviewed Savannah legend Murray Silver, an expert with accolades too many to mention, but among other things wrote *Great Balls of Fire: The Uncensored Story of Jerry Lee*

Lewis, which was adapted to the big screen by Orion Pictures.

Suddenly I was talking about the tour on the show and the show on the tour. It was all good stuff and it all tied into the strangeness that is Savannah. Years of personal experiences, 13 hours of tour material and intriguing guest interviews slowly converged into *Savannah Shadows: Tales from the Midnight Zombie Tour.*

This is for everyone who has taken a Blue Orb tour and joined me as we navigated some of the strangeness that is Savannah.

This book is the rest of the story.

INTRODUCTION ❧

Savannah, Georgia is America's most haunted city. As interest in the paranormal reaches its all-time high, it rightfully sits as the holy Mecca for paranormal enthusiasts.

As millions of people a year journey to Savannah, tour guides have become the paranormal priests. It is from the roving confessional of walking ghost tours that we preach the ghostly gospel. Often, we hear tales from guests never shared with anyone else.

The black clad trustees of Savannah's stories become the lended ear, the soft place to land for those wondering if they are insane or alone in their experience. With few exceptions they are not, and it is from that position of guide and witness that this book is written.

I resisted the temptation to re-tell famous stories better told in better books on the subject. The result would have been a 'Me too' book that would have been unsatisfying, unremarkable and unnecessary.

That is why *Savannah Shadows* goes beyond fundamental. Some of the usual haunts along with their history are covered, but this is not a first reader of Savannah hauntings. Those fine books are the road map. This book is the journey.

This is a book about the people who say they have seen this world meet headlong with the next. It is written for those who have probably had their own brushes with the unknown and have bravely decided to go further. It is for those with "ears to hear" and most importantly, it is for those who love Savannah.

The stories are told primarily from the perspective of the author and

Blue Orb guides on the ground; walking haunted streets, bearing witness to new phenomena and taking you deep into the strange tales from behind the scenes all the way to the doorsteps where they occurred.

It sometimes delves into the modern day personal accounts of others, and therefore, can't be 'goggled'. It references obscure events from antiquity whose only mention was found after digging through the vast archives of the Georgia Historical Society. This book does not attempt to appease the ill-intended critic. Instead, *Savannah Shadows* takes liberties from the norm of apologetics in order to tell the untold.

This book is not without standards though. In fact, they are quite high. As a scientist forms an opinion from analog experiences and countless experiments, this book is crafted upon what has been gathered from touring thousands of guests, conducting hundreds of investigations and having innumerable in-depth conversations with respected and credible icons of the Savannah experience.

At the end of the journey, you will have to draw your own conclusions about these tales. I will offer historical background where relevant and provide supporting materials if they exist, but the course chartered in this book is not mainstream. These stories are firsthand accounts, on the fringe, off to the side and in the shadows. Enjoy.

SECTION ONE ❧ *Provenance*

the WITNESS ✦

I believe every person is born into circumstances over which they have no control. I also believe there are talents bestowed upon us in the same manner. These talents and circumstances, waiting for each of us when we enter life, are at the core of what we mean when we talk about destiny. My destiny, it seems, has always been that of the witness.

In my thirties, I became comfortable with that and began to develop some sense of what it meant. My gift, my destiny, hasn't been getting to *do* or getting to *receive.* Mine has always afforded me the opportunity to get to *see.* I show up right before the *big thing* happens. It happens to someone else; I am just privileged enough to observe it. The value of that became apparent when I attended a book festival where Stephen King was the closing speaker. He said that a writer's job is to bear witness.

However, he also said that occasionally writers have to tell their own story. Occasionally they have to be vulnerable. I felt he was saying, sometimes you have to talk about the big thing that happened to you. He said that part always made him uncomfortable. It resonated with me.

I'm never comfortable talking about myself on a tour. Nevertheless, sometimes you can't avoid it. On the tour I will get the unavoidable questions; "What's the wildest thing that has happened to *you*?" and I know at some point in this book you will rightfully wonder, "So what got *you* into all of this?" Those are fair questions and before I lay bare the stories of others, I feel I should subject myself to the scrutiny first.

The answer to what got me into *all of this* can't be served in one story but I can tell you what got me into Savannah specifically. It happened on a cloudless, winter's day in 2005 when I literally came face to face with something that at the time, at least for me, had no name.

I was in the middle of a successful yet completely unfulfilling career as an engineer with one of the largest telecommunications companies in the world. It's not something I intend to brag about but it was for them, and they constantly made a hell of a big deal about it while reminding us how lucky we were to be parts of it.

In my spare time I was traveling to many haunted cities and locations; doing research, conducting investigations and interviewing witnesses. It was for the love of it, not glory or money. Savannah was a staple stop in those endeavors. I had made some key friendships with people in television and in the paranormal genre and I was glad, honored even, to help.

I was earning a reputation as a go-to person for ethical and reliable data in paranormal investigations. As a solid researcher of history and facts, I began production research for submission to reality paranormal programming.

That is why I have been so hesitant to write what I am about to tell you. I don't want to blow my reputation. I'm already the least credible person in the room because I make a living guiding others through the paranormal and I have everything to gain by creeping you out with a good story. And even as the eyewitness, this still seems altogether unbelievable. Nevertheless, it happened.

and then SHE MELTED ✦

I've always loved the night. As soon as the sun sets, my body seems to calm and I find a special place of concentration that the normal waking hours have never been able to give me. It's when I thrive. Mornings, on the other hand….are hard. Purposely, when I began doing research in Savannah, I did as much as I could under cover of darkness. That would play for a while, but there are archives, storefronts, and people only accessible when the rest of the world is up. January 2005 saw one of those days.

That morning I climbed begrudgingly out of bed and walked onto the balcony of the hotel where I was staying. It felt very early but chilling months like January always make the hours seem younger than they really are. The sun shone full glory but offered no warmth. It was only a gaudy accessory. The morning sky was an unrealistic blue compared to how I had remembered it looking the last time I'd been forced to get up to witness it.

I lit a cigarette and drawing deep, I shied away from them both to stare at the lifeless concrete below. A stout man, a horrible morning person in a drab green maintenance uniform charged ever forward with the leaf blower that a few minutes before had served as my alarm clock. It was much too powerful for the sparse pile of debris it herded into the colorless grass and the perfume of gas carried by light blue smoke reached the second floor balcony. "Fuck." I dropped the practically new cigarette to the ground below, condemning it to an inevitable and futile confrontation with the leaf blower and the son of a bitch wearing it.

Walking back into the room, the carefully cultivated warmth and darkness made me breathe a little easier. Ava, not much better gifted to deal with the horrors of waking early, had a pillow over her head, and murmured something that sounded closely akin to "kill…that…fucker". At 5'3 and 105 lbs., even her profanity laced death threats seemed petite and charming. I smiled as I walked toward the bathroom to shower, grabbing one of her toes quickly as I passed by, pulling until I heard the victorious 'pop'.

The nearly scalding water washed the trauma of morning away and the order of the day began to take shape as I worked out the priorities. First up was the photo shoot. Then notes of each location, along with address, name of current business and an interview with the person on duty (preferably the owner) if possible. Neither of us can eat when we first wake up, regardless of the hour, so I assumed food should come afterward. The rest we would figure out as we went along.

I got out of the shower inspired, and in a much better mood. Naked and vulnerable with wet, *crazy-hair* is usually when I practice my improv and prop comedy. Ava, sleepy and barely amused led me to cut the show short. She was sliding her leather knee boots over her jeans and even with the head start, I still finished getting dressed before her. I sat in the car, letting it warm up until she finally made her way down the stairs. She was wearing a powder blue bowler; a stylish leather jacket in a complicated color a clotheshorse would bristle at my calling "camel" with a complimentary scarf.

We pulled away from the hotel silently and as we made the short drive into town, I concentrated on where to find the elusive parking spot on Bay Street. January paid off and the offseason climate offered me two empty spaces just a few dozen yards from the river. We pulled our gear out of the car and set a tentative game plan. Ava, armed with her camera began to see her "cherry shots" and I could tell she was about to customarily wander off to do her thing. We agreed to canvas a section of Bay and meet back whenever.

I entered shops that looked interesting or familiar and had a few good conversations with proprietors much more willing to talk during the slow season. I'm not sure how much time passed as I walked back towards the car, but synchronicity was at work and Ava was approaching from a side direction. "What are the tunnels?" she asked with obvious interest. She was referring to the River Street side and was looking towards a small tunnel. I knew instantly what she was about to do. "Don't go in there," I warned. "Give me 15 minutes and if I'm not back, come and check on me," she fired back, all the while headed for the tunnel.

I sat on a bench next to a large live oak and began looking over a free map of the city I had gotten from one of the shops. I glanced in the other direction just in time to see Ava make her way towards the river. A few minutes passed and a trolley with less than a dozen people turned onto Bay and the driver's monotone delivery garbled out of the vehicle and onto the street. I glanced up to glare at the mass transit spectacle...and then I saw *it*.

In my periphery, the unmistakable baby blue bowler, the hanging scarf. I did a half glance and said, "How was it?" No response. The powdery blue didn't move. It merely peeked out from behind the live oak. I turned and looked. There was "Ava". Staring, with a twinkling gleam in her eye, but something was amiss. The smile. It wasn't right. It was a half-smile, a semblance. As if you had taken a corpse and tried to forcibly form the upward curve. It was a futile attempt. A smile needs a soul to look genuine. This was a forgery.

I stared, but did not speak. There was no need. Deep down, I knew it wouldn't have responded and I'm not sure I could have. It stared at me and the smile began to draw downward as if it were something that had never known the natural path of smile muscles. It had never had a body of its own and could only form a dull conjuration. I felt my arm hair stand as it reacted to the electricity coming from it, the hate. The face began to distort. It was losing the ability to hold its form. It began to sink slowly behind the live oak. It saw the disbelief on my face and the beginnings of something, perhaps a laugh, came out of it as a quick guttural rattling. And it was gone.

For the first time in my life, I could not move voluntarily. It wasn't fear. It was clinical shock. Lay him on his back and elevate his legs, shock. It could have only lasted an instant but it felt much slower. My mind raced so fast it gave the illusion that time slowed down. It stopped. I had, in an instant, time to reflect. I knew I had to make a decision to either go into full-blown panic or try to pull out of it. I don't remember how much time passed, or the thoughts I had between, but my next conscious memory saw me standing. I could not look behind the live oak. It's fucking broad daylight and I couldn't even go near it. Then I saw Ava.

She was walking back up the small hill toward me on Bay Street. She was looking at the previewer on her camera and that is about all I remember. We had a conversation when she saw me. In hindsight, I've relied on her memory of what I said and how I acted. The words "pale", "despondent" and "confused" were all in her description. I remember burping quite a bit. I'm not sure if I hyperventilated or had a panic attack but I felt like I was full of air and kept burping as I tried to breathe normally.

When I look back on that event, I wonder what had traumatized me besides the obvious. After many years of doing this I have seen some incredible things. Things we don't post on our websites because with the advent of Photoshop most people would be unable to believe it and chalk it up as hyperbole to sell a tour or a book.

I had spent my whole life asking, what can you show me? I've always been a searcher. I had a habit of working long enough to save up for my next adventure and then driving ever forward into it. In 1996, I had been in Israel and Jordan, in later years Haiti and Jamaica. I had seen things that even with witnesses in tow, would have made my mother call me a full-fledged space bunny, but this was different. This was personal. This thing wasn't something I happened to be in the right place at the right time to witness. This thing came at me in the form of someone I knew. It was peeking at **me**. Spying on **me**. Fucking with **me**.

Time has passed and I have revisited that strange spot. The grass still grows there. Flowers still bloom. There is no eternal cold. It looks absolutely normal. I have no witnesses. No video footage. No EMF readings. It just came and went and that was it. I have only my jumbled memory of the events and the cautious belief that I am generally sane and not delusional.

I haven't looked at daylight the same since. Spirits were no longer just on the graveyard shift, at least not in Savannah. It would be a year before I knew what to call this thing. It would be months before I would even tell anyone else besides Ava.

I had just met *The Hag*.

ATLANTA ✈

Finding a way to lose time is a powerful coping mechanism. It can allow you to escape the horrific, or cause you to neglect the things that matter. Some do it with a hobby or with alcohol. For me, it has always been my job.

When I returned to my position as a project manager and engineer, the company I worked for was in full swing deploying the equipment that makes fast access internet possible. It wasn't long before I had enough work to occupy my time and take my thoughts off what happened in Savannah.

I wasn't necessarily trying to forget. However, I did need some time to *towel off.* I needed to process it; decide if I could integrate it into my version of reality. Being single with no children leaves you with a lot of free time when you aren't at work.

A solitary life is a self-absorbed existence and with no one to care about but myself I was at liberty to wallow in my thoughts and make the memory as horrible as I wanted. And that's exactly what I did. For months, I turned away from research, from Savannah and from investigations.

Then later that year, something happened that made me have to deal with it. Savannah came to me through an odd and chance phone call, spilling over into my day in a way that would be hard not to describe as, *Fate.*

You see, part of my job as a project manager was to meet deadlines. I had started as a technician so I understood what the people who reported to me did. It was one of the reasons I was successful as a project manager.

The other reason was, I'm from the south. (You will understand what I mean by that in just a moment.)

The nine state region we serviced essentially comprised the Southeast. Being from Alabama…I'm a *local.* On the rare event I had to speak with a field technician to troubleshoot a project that was flirting with a missing deadline, I had at least a semblance of the same weird accent as the tech in a place like Kentucky. Or the one from Raleigh, who a few moments before had become frustrated and hung up on my colleague in our Atlanta office that was from Nigeria or India or God forbid, up north.

I could relate to the guys who were late for "supper" because the "goddamn shit" wouldn't work while they stood in the freezing dark in Asheville. I knew what the field tech in Mobile meant when he said "coldbeer" as a single word and lamented that it was past time for one. I knew if I were asked if I liked "real-good-pizza" to respond with "Hell, if I can find it." It was rhetorical, and followed by a suggestion of where to get it when I next found myself in Birmingham or Memphis. And so it was the day the easy-paced field tech from Savannah fell out with the loud, urgent engineer from Connecticut, that I was called in to mediate.

It was the end of the month…crunch time in the corporate world. We were also approaching the holidays and most people who had saved their vacation were using it or losing it. We were a skeleton crew but with the same amount of work. We were *in the weeds.* The Savannah central office, that remote location technology filters down to before it reaches your neighborhood and eventually your home, was in the same predicament.

Our Atlanta office had been troubleshooting an issue for half the day. Tensions were high, nerves were thin and it was time to go home but that couldn't happen until the equipment was up and running. I had a brief conversation with our tech then called the central office.

In Savannah, an already tense voice answered the phone. I knew he was going to have to vent before we could troubleshoot. I set it up for him to knock it down and gave him permission to let it all out with a five-word question: "What's wrong with that thing?" There was barely a pause before he shot back, "This Alcatel shit ain't fit for fire starter, that's what's wrong."

Alcatel is based in France.

For ten minutes, I listened to what was wrong with French equipment and France in general...how we had saved them from extinction twice in the twentieth century and how ungrateful they were. I listened to how "the last ol' boy" he had talked to would be without hope should he ever need to differentiate between his ass and a hole in the ground. I took it in stride and slowed the cadence of my inflection to match *my raisin'* until eventually he grew calm.

Finally, we began troubleshooting and the first bright spot showed itself as two of the four lights that were red, turned glorious green. "I have sync on two ports." I said excitedly. "I see em' too." He shot back. I could hear the tension leave him as he said it and though he would still be begrudging France, at least we would all be home in time for *supper.*

"My damn dog is gonna bite me if I get home this early," he said laughing. (For my friends in France and the greater Connecticut area, he meant his dog will not be expecting him home this early and will probably mistake him for an intruder.)

The conversation was winding down nicely and visions of the weekend danced in my head...but then came the comment that gut punched me. You know the kind, like when you hear the ex you still have it for is dating again and doing just fine...that kind of gut punch.

I listened as he started laughing uneasily, "Savannah has a lot of damn problems, now I'm starting to think we have a ghost too." I laughed with him and said, "Well, you are in America's most haunted city." He paused, "That's what I keep hearin'. I transferred here from Vidalia, Georgia but these guys in here are convinced we got one."

He wasn't joking.

I paused long enough to consider the options. Do I go deeper or do I play it cool and get off the line? Well...you know damn well what I did.

"Why do they think that?" I inquired. "Well, we keep having issues with these cards," he started, "weird stuff. Like comin' in and all the cards have been disconnected or pulled halfway out of their slots. We even told security about it but they say the alarm never goes off...still, there's no way this stuff is happening by itself. Those cards are damn hard to pull out once they're snapped in place."

"Is there a camera in that office?" I asked hoping. "Nah, not in this one...well, there's one in the parking lot but not in the office. We got one guy here who actually put 'ghost' on a trouble ticket. (More laughter)

Nobody thought anything of it Tobias, but I swear he was serious."

I knew he was ready to go home but to leave something this intriguing would have been torturous so I cut the foreplay. "Well, what do **you** think?" I asked bluntly. "Iiiii don't know. I don't really belief in that stuff…but it's weird. The one guy, Gary, says it the most but he is a shiftless sonofabitch, so I just figured he was bullshittin'….a ton a people who stay in the office more than me believe it. I work out in the field, mostly."

This was all the help he would be. I decided to end the conversation and let him face his unsuspecting dog while I faced my last memory of Savannah. "Ok, buddy. Well I'm glad we have everything working. Maybe the goblins will leave it alone this time," I said with finality and he agreed.

After I got off the call, I sat and thought about what he had said. Talking about ghosts in Savannah is like talking about weed in Amsterdam so I didn't want to take this too personally. Something told me this had substance, though, and even if it wasn't *Fate*, I felt it was certainly a sign. I had been given the nudge I needed to examine this a little closer.

I logged into several different systems to look at data for different areas, including Savannah. I had access to deployment data, trouble ticket history, and the average time to complete trouble issues, complete with technician notes for the entire region. In the engineering world, it is called (appropriately) "Historical data". We worked with so many cities and had so many project managers it would be difficult to discern a pattern in any one place unless someone did what I was doing…and there it was.

Savannah was awash in red. Missed due dates. Late deployments. Four and half times more trouble tickets than the next closest city of its size. And then, there were the odd technician notes. I confirmed things like *"Unexplained surge to board." "Cards cracked". "Card missing from slot." "Circuit wire melted but voltage normal."*

The tickets went on and on and they were definitely not the kind I was used to seeing. Typically, a problem would be listed as *"Bad card upon arrival." "Replaced cable."* Reasonable things like that.

I didn't need to look at this from a paranormal enthusiast's standpoint. I had been with fast-access deployment since 2000. I could see it just fine from a project manager's. I knew what was industry-normal. This was not.

By now, it was pushing 7 p.m. and I was tired and hungry. I had taken in all I could for the moment. I would have the weekend to play it back in my mind and decide what it meant but there wasn't much suspense in it for me. I know myself and I knew where this was leading. I was going back to Savannah.

DECEMBER ✤

Before heading to Savannah, I had to get through the holidays. They were largely uneventful but it did give me a chance to slow down and reconnect with my old research partner.

Mark is from my hometown in Alabama. He's the reclusive genius type. Usually, I can only find him by driving home and asking one of his brothers where he might be. This time I found him living in a mobile home. His place was a wreck. One room was full of desktop computers he had collected as throw-aways by their owners. They were lying on the floor, gutted for the gold that could be harvested from their motherboards. Rare books on alchemy and conspiracy surrounded him predictably. Half-completed registration forms for gold mining memberships lay at his feet. I didn't dare put my keys down for fear of not being able to find them again.

We stepped outside so he could show me his compost heap and where his first attempt at organic growing would be, come planting season. He talked about certain spiders and the way their webs naturally protected crops. We talked about how valuable gold was right now and had a conversation about the Anasazi Indians, speculating as to what had driven them to eventually live in nearly inaccessible caves on the sides of deadly desert mountains, and which moon of Jupiter we though held the most promise for primitive life...the usual stuff.

Mark is an easy friend and a Minuteman for the Apocalypse. I knew it wouldn't take much prodding to talk him into a road trip. He could always leave at the drop of a hat and wouldn't need an explanation as to why I had to go back to Savannah. I laid out the plan and told him it would have to be at the first of the year when I had a fresh infusion of vacation days. He agreed with no questions and the trip was set.

HUM *of the* BAYS ✢

It was January and Mark had a job washing cabs but because he had such a hard time being around people, he washed them at night in near freezing cold and in a very questionable part of town. He also liked cleaning at night because he could get quick dibs on any valuables left inside before the usually intoxicated passengers sobered up and tried to reclaim them the next day. I was curious why he had wanted me to pick him up at work but I don't ask him questions either.

I pulled up about 2 a.m. and Mark was inside a cab. The vacuum was making a tremendous amount of noise so I sat in the car, smoking while I waited. He noticed my headlights and hurried to finish before stepping into the cabstand to collect his pay (in cash), then told them he was quitting. I only overheard part of the conversation but I had seen Mark quit jobs before so I was able to fill in the blanks. He took off the wet coveralls and tossed them into a small, weathered duffle bag and picked up his plastic bag of stray cigarettes, money and all of the assorted treasure found under the seats of numerous cabs after a busy Friday night.

He climbed into the car, lit a found cigarette, and plugged his early generation iPod into my stereo. I remember how excited he had been the night the iPod had been left in the cab-van. The vans always held the most promise for choice scores.

I told him I thought he liked the cab job and I was surprised he would quit just to go to Savannah for a few days. "I'll get the job back after we come back. Nobody wants that shit job."

We listened to classic episodes of *Coast to Coast* with Art Bell on the iPod for most of the trip. We critiqued the kooky callers during the open line segments and drove into a foggy and cold Savannah about 8 a.m.

After breakfast at Clary's Café, we wandered around Savannah to kill a few hours before we could check into the hotel. As we entered one of the nearby shops, I noticed Mark reach for a free map from the counter. My mind immediately flashed back to the melting face I had seen almost exactly a year before.

There isn't much going on in Savannah in January. We walked down River Street, then Bay Street and finally we stood in front of *the tree.* I went into detail with him about what had happened there a year before. He listened intently as I reenacted the events as they had unfolded to the best of my memory. Then I then told him about the conversation I had with the technician...the conversation that had brought us to Savannah that day. "Do you know where the office he was calling from is?" Mark asked calmly. "Yeah, sure," I said. "Well, why don't we go there and talk to the guy he said had witnessed so much stuff...the shiftless guy."

Secretly, I hoped he would suggest that but I knew I had to be careful. It was one thing to take a friendly ribbing from co-workers about my keen interest in the paranormal and my hobby of pursuing it vigorously in my free time, but it was another matter entirely to mix that world with my career. This couldn't get back to my office in Atlanta.

We walked back to the car. As I navigated a city full of squares, round-abouts and one-way streets, we talked about the best way to approach the guy. As we reached the address, I saw that the building was secure. You needed an activated identification badge to enter and a security gate surrounded the parking lot. This wasn't unusual as most central offices are tightly controlled because of the expensive equipment they contain.

I was tempted to let this be my reason for abandoning the effort but I knew neither my conscience nor Mark would allow it. It was an easy fix. I had all the major offices in my phone so I pulled up the main Savannah number and armed with only a first name, I made the call.

The technician that answered the phone spoke loudly over the equipment hum in the background. I had to repeat the technician's name I wanted to speak with twice before he understood me. "Hold on," he said abruptly. Less than a minute later Gary answered with the same hurried, loud voice.

NOTICE

You are leaving the U.S.
You are entering the Yoruba Kingdom

In the name of His
Highness Efuntola, peace
welcome to the sacred
Yoruba village of Oyotunji.
The only village in North America
built by priests of the
Vodun cults as a tribute to
our ancestors These priests
preserve the customs, law
and religion of the African race
Welcome to ourland!

It took several minutes for me to get him to understand I wasn't making a service call and even after I related how I came to know his name there was still the awkward missing piece of the conversational puzzle... why was I calling. Out of sheer desperation I was almost overt with my core question which would have been, *"Hey, I saw a shape shifter a year ago and I think you may be able to help me get some shit worked out."*

Fortunately, calm sank in and what could have sounded like the ramblings of a madman, came out (in a surprisingly calm voice), "Hey, I'm in Savannah for a few days and I was wondering if I could talk to you about some of the deployment issues your office is having?" I glanced at Mark and he stared back with silent approval and a slight nod to my approach. "Yeah that's fine. You wanna just come to the gate and I'll sign you in?" He replied without hesitation. "Sure. I can be there in five."

We pulled up to the gate. The sign in process was less formal than I imagined. The technician we met handed us a clipboard and offered each of us a Vendor badge as we followed him through the long bays of equipment. The hum of technology had been too loud for a proper greeting when we signed in; it wasn't until we arrived at a small back office that I was sure we had found the right person.

He closed the door, which shut out most of the noise, and we exchanged introductions. "So what brings ya'll to Savannah?" he asked as he checked his phone then swirled his chair around to check his email. "Gimme one second, here," he said as he put the phone to his ear.

My eyes wandered around the office as I observed well known deployment and territory maps. The conversation was familiar as well. The field tech he was speaking with apparently had a software issue. The card he had installed was not recognizing it. It didn't surprise me. The latest software was released with a lot of bugs and we were seeing the same issues in Atlanta.

Gary recommended that the field technician install the old software version on the card first and then the new version and then delete the old. It was obvious Gary had been seeing this issue quite a bit lately because we were using the same fix in Atlanta.

"Alright, sorry about that," Gary said as he swiveled around and leaned forward to face us. "No, problem," I said. "That new software is for shit," he said convincingly. I knew we could easily get off-track bemoaning the new software for all its faults so I moved right into the purpose for my visit.

"Gary, I've heard you folks are having some strange issues here. Like the kind of issues that are really hard to explain." He gave a quick smile and interlocked his hands. He looked like he was on a witness stand and his expression said this had gone from conversation to interview. I watched his brow and forehead move while he considered his response.

(Nervous laughter) "Yeah, we've had a few strange things," he confided. I needed to let him know he was in a safe place and speaking to a soft audience if I expected him to be honest so I took the lead, "I have been looking at the trouble tickets here and I see some very odd patterns as well." I couldn't tell if that made him feel more comfortable or defensive so I decided to go a little further. "The reason I am down here, is because I am wondering if you think it might be, well…paranormal," I asked sheepishly. "Oh man, that's exactly what I was afraid you were going to ask me. Are ya'll here to haul me off?" He said, laughing.

Body language says it all in an interview, especially when you are speaking with someone about paranormal activity. They need to think you might be crazy before they can be comfortable saying things that might make you think that they are. "Let's step out back. I need a cigarette for this," Gary said as he reached for his phone and led us back through the loud hum of equipment bays and took a sharp right that led out the back door.

He lit the cigarette and put one foot flat against the wall behind him. He leaned into it as he took a short, nervous puff. "Ok, I'll tell you, I don't know what the hell is going on. But it's somethin'." I refrained from responding to Gary's vague answer and instead looked at him expectantly. I wanted him to speak on it and be honest about what he thought might be going on, specifically what was happening.

"This building we in now? We hadn't been here just a little while… you know, once the DSL (Digital Subscriber Line or non-dial up internet) really started takin off…that's when we opened this office and that's when it all started. Things movin', cards flying out of the holding slots. These cards here, they're clamped in. They can't just fly out," Gary paused as if he needed affirmation before he would go any further.

"Have you ever seen this happen?" I asked. "Yeah I have and if you say I said it, I'll call ya a liar," Gary answered nervously. "I've seen cards fly out of bays and I've seen the shadows of people walking between the bays when no one was here but me. No offense, man, but I'll call you a liar if you say I said it. These guys here already give me shit, but they ain't here when I am."

"I'm not gonna say a damn thing, Gary. I just want to know what's going on. That's the reason we're down here. I had an experience in Savannah last year. I've been doing paranormal research for a pretty good while, but I still can't explain what happened to me."

I was now officially crazier than he was. "You mean like ghost hunters?" He asked curiously with a slight but interested grin. "Yeah, like ghost hunters I guess; mainly any mysterious occurrence. Not just ghosts. I guess you could say I'm a searcher."

"So, how did you get into that?" Gary replied. (Since a goodly portion of this book deals with how I got "into that", I will refrain from retyping it here). Suffice it to say, I took Gary through a brief timeline of the things that got me interested enough in the paranormal to pursue it on my own dime. Actually, I was glad to do it. It caused him to forget to ask what happened to me in Savannah for the time being and that was fine by me.

"I know several people that are into that stuff. Savannah is the place to do it. Hell, they need to come investigate this place but I know we could never let them." Gary focused the conversation back on himself and Savannah. "Since we have started running these lines we have found bones in the ground and trees; hell, this whole place is full of dead folks."

"But I'll tell you the creepiest damn thing. Hell, I'll just let you listen to it." Gary pulled out his phone and began looking through it. After several minutes I became convinced he wasn't setting us up. He was much too disorganized and for a few moments I thought we might just have to settle for him telling us what he was going to have shown us.

"Here it is. Listen to this." Gary put the phone up to my ear and the hum from the equipment bay was immediately clear as a bell. I heard him talking "Test...test...test 1-2," then another voice, *"Tha train hit me."* Gary pulled the phone away and looked at me expectantly. "The train hit me" I repeated. "Yes! Thank you! I didn't even have to tell you, it's plain as day itn't it?" he exclaimed.

"When did you pick that up?" I asked. "A few months ago. Freaky as hell itn't it? I had my phone turned on and I was testing the voice recorder. When I played it back, that was on there." Gary talked willingly now and at a fevered pace. "You know what else is freaky as hell? Guess what used to be just over there?" Gary pointed in a general direction; "Train tracks. My granddaddy said hobos used to hop trains and sometimes they would pass out drunk on the tracks or get killed trying to jump on one as it passed."

I looked at Mark. "What do you think?" I asked. "Well, it makes sense. And this whole damn place is a white noise conductor with those service bays," Mark said plainly. "White noise? What do you mean?" asked Gary.

"Well there are a lot of different theories but a large number of frequencies emitting at once is believed to cause ambient sounds to be drowned out. Like when you use a fan to fall asleep; to drown out voices or other noise. Some theories say that the white noise is conducive to picking up the voices of the dead or even causing manifestations. I've seen white noise generators used at places where investigations had taken place previously. It took the investigation from fruitless to producing visually unaided sightings. The only difference was the introduction of white noise." I could see Mark's monotone and articulate answer had peaked Gary's interest. "Do you think that's why I have seen those shadows?" Gary asked, staring hard at Mark.

"It's quite possible. You're the one in there the most. You're the one in there at night. I'd be willing to bet if we put someone else in your place, they would have similar experiences." Mark's response seemed to put Gary at ease.

"Well hell, at least I know I'm not crazy. I haven't let anyone listen to that," Gary said. "I'd hold onto it. You may even want to bring a recorder to work and try it out from time to time," I said seriously. "Nah, I don't wanna fool with that stuff. I just wanted to know I'm not crazy," Gary shook his head.

We had reached the end of the conversation and he walked us back to the front, taking our badges and signing us out. We said goodbye and thanked him for his time and openness in speaking with us.

As we pulled out of the driveway, Mark looked at me and said, "You have to move here. Your experience, his experience…that's just the tip of it. You wanted to do research full time. Well, here it is. New Orleans is too far, Franklin is too small and this is the best place we've been so far. Every time we come to Savannah, it pays off. You need to pull the trigger and come here. The rest will work its self out."

Whether Gary was out of his mind or not, I knew Mark was right. I had to come. And I believed the rest *would* work its self out.

In the years that followed, I returned to Savannah often and continued my research. I attempted to transfer with my company but my skill set was best served in Atlanta.

I finally made the decision to relocate to Savannah after taking an early buy out option from my employer. I worked with several people in Savannah on various projects until I decided to start Blue Orb Tours in January 2010.

Section 2 begins a collection of things I, and many with me, have witnessed while dealing with the low country conjuring community in the years leading up to starting Blue Orb and since.

SECTION TWO ✦ *The Conjurer Speaks*

criss-CROSS ✈

G hosts versus Zombies. It sounds like a terrible B horror movie that I would be all over at 2 a.m. on a Thursday but it's not. It is unwittingly the dividing line between paranormal schools of thought in Savannah. Everyone who visits is exposed to the *ghost* or colonial version of why the city is so haunted. The mainstream version.

However, there is another side. The silent contributors to our phenomena. The Conjurers version. The 'zombie' version.

When I arrived in Savannah I was a tourist, a traveler and a researcher. I explored all the sights, took advantage of the open container law, and properly defiled myself in all the traditional endeavors. I also went on plenty of tours.

I found an abundance of them (47 at last count), and despite what some rival companies might say about their counterparts, the overwhelming majority of owners are doing their best to give the traveler a premium experience. Most of them are succeeding. Nevertheless, respectfully, I did see a gap.

I wanted to bring information to the paranormal table that had yet to gain focus within the existing tours in the city. No costumes, no pirate accents and no special effects. All of which are a blast with the right formula of alcohol and friends, but I wanted Blue Orb to talk about the things I had wondered when I came here as a traveler. Things I had to search for myself between visits. I wanted to deliver it in an uncensored fashion and in the style of classic storytelling. I wanted to get to a different part of the meat of Savannah.

I envisioned a marriage between *Colonial Savannah* and *Conjurering Savannah*. The resulting effort would become our flagship tour: The Midnight Zombie Tour.

I took the jokes in stride when some established tour operators poked a little good fun at the word 'zombie' being in the title. It was harmless, but it did confirm my conviction that there was a whole genre of paranormal Savannah that was so foreign that even some tour operators didn't get it.

Their concept of the word zombie had been shaped by media culture, and I think John Stephens accurately pointed it out in his book *Voodoo*; the media culture adopted it primarily from *The Magic Island* by William Seabrook published in 1929. While Seabrook's zombie was a sensational and fantastically fun idea, it is not the correct concept in authentic Hoodoo and Voodoo beliefs. In its original form, zombie is an interchangeable word for "ghost or spirit". Voodoo culture in particular, teaches of both spiritual and physical zombies.

With that focus in mind, my research grew from my experiences in Haiti and Jamaica, as well as the Savannah low country. It pulled me away from the Savannah founded in 1733. For me, hauntings could no longer start and stop with the mainstream tales of tragic events that occurred in 200-year-old buildings on any given street in the Historic District.

As wonderful and intriguing as those are, the stories that live in Savannahs shadows don't just reside on streets like West *Oglethorpe*. They hail from places like West *Africa* and their beginnings are as old as mankind.

Once you step onto that ancient path, you have to temporarily lay down words like *paranormal* and *ghosts* and pick up words like *JuJu* and *zombies*. You have to get comfortable with the idea that Christianity isn't the only belief with a Trinity. For example, Stephens points out in *Voodoo*, "the Father, Son and Holy Ghost become The Loa, The Twins and The Dead". It is widely known that both Hoodoo and Voodoo incorporated many parts of Christianity into their belief systems when they arrived.

Once the *JuJu* settled in Savannah it split into two distinct but generally inseparable versions:

✤ *HooDoo*, Conjuh and *Obeah* (Generally considered the dark sorcery variety of Conjuh).

Later, the intermingling of slaves crossing paths in transit eventually also brought:

✦ Vodun/Voodoo

While you would get lost trying to divide which is which in every case, there are distinct differences and many misconceptions.

Savannah and the outlying low country contain both varieties of practitioners. Overall, you would not be ill-served by thinking of New Orleans as the seat of Voodoo in the United States; while Savannah as the seat of Hoodoo. Let's not get too meticulous on this point but it is a good way to get a general feel for the migration of each.

In general, Voodoo deals with the entire community and focuses on everything as a whole. People who practice it usually do so as a way of life. While it is also a religion, Voodoo adherents see Voodoo at work in everything in much the same way Christians might see God or Christ at work in all aspects of life.

In general, Hoodoo focuses on empowering the individual rather than the community. One aspect of Hoodoo is *Obeah* which might be used for individual protection or to increase personal wealth, power, healing, success in business or…revenge.

When Hoodoo turns dark, as into the realm of revenge on others, it takes on the mood of esoteric sorcery. Many of the rituals call for making a doll, or semblance of the intended target. This actually began as an Obeah/Hoodoo practice, although the Voodoo would later incorporate it.

My journeys brought me face to face with both religions in Savannah. It irrevocably shaped my attitude about how they contributed to the crown jewel of haunted cities and they were taking me to the outer limits of the low country and onto the unlit paths.

voodoo NATION ➤

The curious Voodoo settlement of Oyotunji is located about 50 miles outside of Savannah. It was founded by Oba Efuntola Oseijeman Adelabu Adefunmi, whose original name was Walter Eugene King. His surname was serendipitous as he would be the first king of Oyotunji.

According to my guide at the village, the king was born in 1928 and was the first American ever initiated into the organized Vodun religion of Africa. By that act, he is considered a legitimate king (Oba) in Voodoo practice. My research indicates he was, in fact ordained by the Vodun kings of Nigeria in 1981, complete with a coronation. He also studied Voodoo extensively in Haiti in the 1950's.

Under his rule, Oyotunji was established as a Voodoo settlement, a holy nation, and does not consider itself a part of the United States. The village drew criticism and fear from locals for instituting the Egungun Masquerade (a dress festival for The Dead), as well as, the Secret Society.

The Vodun nation is now ruled by King Adenfuni II, the first king's fourteenth son. Oyotunji has remained a paradox. At times, it has been seen as a foreboding place where even outside conjurers don't roam. A local EMT told me, they were not allowed to go inside when the first king died. Instead, his body was carried to the entrance of the settlement.

Other times, it presents a caracuture of itself with tribal music festivals including visitors that wreak of stinky, high grade marijuana with a sign on the main road that advertises the Vodun Villlage "As seen on T.V.". This is in reference to the first Oba's appearance on *The Oprah Winfrey Show.*

My first visit to the settlement was by chance, December 21, which was the winter solstice. It was also the birthday of King Adenfunmi II. I woke early enough that morning to make the nearly one hour drive to the settlement. I followed the directions into Sheldon, South Carolina and eventually saw the small dirt road that leads to Oyotunji.

As I advanced, the small tight rows of compacted earth from the previous week's rain began to shake and rattle my car. I noticed immediately how dark it became as I traveled deeper. Even in the winter, the Live Oak coverage is foreboding. I passed several older homes, unaffiliated with Oyotunji and as I rounded a sharp curve, there it was.

I was immediately awe-struck by miniature castle-like walls built around the settlement, and a hand painted sign that read, "You are now leaving the United States…the only village in the United States built by priests of the Vodun cults." I felt a heavy silence as I approached the front gate and passed a few goats tied with old rope to a large tree. Seeing no one in sight, I slowly ventured across the threshold onto the property of Oyotunji, and in their minds, *out* of the United States.

I wondered if the U.S. government was aware the settlement did not consider itself a part of this country. I concluded they must live quietly with no visible stockpile of weapons so even if the government knew, they concluded the village posed no threat. However, it was not the sign's declaration that gave me pause as I stepped onto their land, rather it was the spiritual presence I experienced.

Standing on this odd property, surrounded by nothing but dense winter woods save a few sacrificial goats, I was completely alone. Yet I had the undeniable feeling of being watched. I walked further in and saw two men dressed in white robes walking calmly, but deliberately towards me.

We met in the center of, what I suppose, would have been the town square. I tried to appear as humble and nonthreatening as possible. I politely introduced myself and concisely explained my request, "I was wondering if it would be possible for me to meet with the king?" Their looks bordered on *marveling* upon hearing my request. I had obviously asked a great thing.

There didn't appear to be anyone else present, much less King Oba Adefunmi II. When they asked me why I wanted to meet with him, I revealed my fascination with the village and desire to know if it was open to outsiders. More importantly, would they ever consider letting tour groups explore with a guide.

They didn't balk at my statement, as I assumed. Instead they walked away hurriedly saying they would make a phone call. I waited several tense minutes and was beyond surprised to learn the king would meet with me. As the conversation progressed, I learned the good fortune of my arrival on the winter solstice and the king's birthday. There was a celebration later in the day for his highness and I could meet with him before the festivities. The anticipation on my face was obvious as the man looked me up and down decidedly and said, "Be back at 1:30." I readily agreed and with several hours to kill, I was determined to have a look around the rest of the Sheldon area before returning.

As I made the drive back to the main road, I couldn't help but wonder what the king would be like. There were two hundred families at the settlement and at least two nations in Africa recognizing this man as a legitimate king.

At the main highway, I turned in the opposite direction and after a few miles, I saw a produce stand which was more of a small house really. It advertised apple cider, jams and jellies. I pulled into the small parking lot, made my way up to the porch thru a screen door, and took a step back in time. The place was full of sweets from every conceivable local fruit. Organic syrups were housed next to homemade banana bread, sodas in glass bottles, and of course the cider.

As I looked around, a large portly woman came out of the back and asked if she could help me. I explained I was just looking, but since I was the only customer in the store, after an uncomfortable silence I decided to ask her about Oyotunji. She looked surprised and proclaimed she didn't know much about the settlement but I should talk to the baker. She seemed disturbed by my question and I got the distinct feeling she wasn't being perfectly honest with me. She walked to the back, presumably to get the baker.

After several minutes, a woman in a white jacket and hairnet appeared from the back wiping her hands into a towel. She looked as if she had already been briefed as to why I was there. "Why is it you want to know?" She asked. I explained I owned a tour company in Savannah and I was hoping to generate some interest in the settlement. I expressed my own interest and told her I thought others would share it if they had the opportunity.

She shook her head in disapproval before I could even finish the idea. "I don't think you should take people to that place. If you want to tour people somewhere up here, take them to the Sheldon Church ruins. It was burned by both the English during the Revolutionary war and by Sherman during his march to the sea," she said proudly. "Yes, I have heard of the Sheldon Church ruins but I haven't been there," I said, trying to sound interested. She seemed relieved and eagerly elaborated on the finer points of its mass appeal.

Despite her efforts, I couldn't let it go. I wanted to know any strange stories, wild rumors or verifiable events of the fantastic. I was extremely curious to know what a mostly white, mostly Christian, mostly southern population would have to say about a place as bold as Oyotunji.

I suggested my question to her again and she saw I wasn't going to relent. She let the energy of her frustration allow her to be honest. "They're not Christians," she started. "They practice witchcraft, they practice Voodoo, and everyone in the area is leery of them. I don't think they pay their taxes, they work with stucco and they travel to places like Canada...I'm assuming that's so they won't have to report any income. There are a lot of people buried there; people that helped build it mostly. I know they buy goats and they use them in sacrifices *and* they are grave robbers. I wish they would go away."

I was amused at her transparent animosity and fear toward these people. I was entertained with her contradictory statements and simple prejudices. I didn't know where to start. I considered asking her if she was aware money made outside of the United States doesn't have to be taxed...or suggesting many people do similar things by working in war zones like Iraq and Afghanistan. I decided I wasn't there to defend Oyotunji or a free market economy. We had come to the end of our common ground and it was time for me to buy something and go.

In Haiti and Jamaica the offering of fruit, produce and meat are considered proper gifts. Knowing it was the winter solstice as well as the king's birthday, I thought it would be a good idea for me to take an offering back with me when I met him in the afternoon.

I considered telling them what my purchases were for but thought better of it. I assembled a basket of assorted jellies and a large glass jug of apple cider and bid them farewell. As I started out the door one of the women said, "You aren't going there are you?" Again, my higher judgment prevailed and I simply said I was headed to the church. "Oh good you will really enjoy that," she said warmly.

It wasn't actually a lie. I still had some time to kill and I was going to visit the church ruins. It would give me a little time to think about what I wanted to say and how best to portray myself to the king.

As I drove down the newly paved and tightly curved highway, I observed the infinite brown signs alerting the traveler to the approaching church ruins. It was beyond overkill and I had to wonder if the folks in the area had a *No, no, don't go to Oyotunji, go here instead!* attitude or if I was just being paranoid because of my previous rebuke at the jelly, jam and jargon place.

There is a small parking lot across the street from the ruins. The road is unusually busy for a two-lane highway in the middle of nowhere. I had to pull into the driveway hastily in order to escape the horn of displeasure from motorists traveling at break-neck speeds from the other direction.

I immediately noted two caretakers raking leaves near the entrance. As I got out the car, they stopped raking to stare. I nodded at them but they did not return the greeting. I had to wait nearly a minute before I had a clear shot across the dangerous road. It felt like a human version of *Frogger* but as I saw the ancient graveyard full of misaligned headstones, it took on more of a *Pet Sematary* vibe.

The graves were plentiful and from many different eras. The first ones I came upon were neatly arranged in a formal burial area but beyond those, I saw others scattered throughout the wooded area around the church. It was obvious this had been a grand place and even the burned-out shell still seemed impressive.

I walked onto the slab of the foundation. Huge pieces of wall, the kind you wish could talk, were all around me as I made my way to where the pulpit must have been located.

The frightened, irrational prejudice towards Oyotunji, the obstinate advocacy for Sheldon Church and the two nosy, antisocial assholes with rakes had caused me to enter the property cross. As I stood at the burned out altar, I made my peace with the church and forgave the trespasses against my sensibility. Its hauntingly beautiful presence had won me over.

Cleansed, I was free to become curiously intrigued with the small details of the holy place. I imagined the different congregations that had come and gone, the fiery sermons to keep faith even as reports of the coming British became more numerous, the community meetings convened there as defeat became imminent. I made my way past the large fireplace and wondered what it would have been like to attend church when roaring fires set the mood for winter sermons full of brimstone and played the backdrop for passionate pleas to stay vigilant as Sherman's fire drew ever closer that cold winter of 1864.

I had stayed at Sheldon, stuck in time longer than I had intended. I looked at my watch and realized 1:30 was close enough to make my way back to Oyotunji. As I parked next to the small fortified wall, I entered a magical place. There was no denying the energy. It was the same feeling I had gotten the first time I visited Haiti. It was not danger or evil...it was more like an overwhelming realization I was merely a guest in a very unpredictable world compared to my own.

The scene was far different from the one I had left only hours before. There were almost a dozen cars in the parking lot and a bustle of activity. Everyone was dressed in white...except me. I was wearing my customary black, adding another layer of oddity to my already out of place appearance.

I made my way toward the crowd and tried to locate one of the two gentlemen I had spoken with earlier. I could not remember what they looked like distinctly and foolishly, I hadn't taken into consideration the combined event would surely draw a crowd.

I nodded at those who were willing and my eyes were drawn to a bright yellow door in the market square. Painted in a rough low country font, the words *House of Magic* were emblazoned in green. I pushed the door open gently and as soon as my interest was perceived, a woman in white was quick to step into the room.

I was eager to do anything that might soften the contrast of my presence from the rest of the revelers. I looked for something to purchase and eventually became interested in some powder that promised to return any love I had lost. I asked the woman behind the counter how to acti-

vate the powder and she informed me there were instructions on the back. I turned the packet over and among the miniscule type; I read the ritual must be performed during the waxing moon with the recitation of the spell to be spoken at its conclusion.

Ultimately, I was drawn to the masks and the iron instruments of war and magic lying against the wall next to handmade bowls and rusty daggers. I inquired as to the origin of a few of the items and it became apparent everything in this room was genuine. Some of the items sold for several hundred dollars, while others demanded a price of several thousand. I bought the $3 *Return to Me Powder*. I wasn't sure why I picked it. I didn't want any of my *exes* back. I didn't see any *Go Away Powder* though, and concluded it was probably on backorder.

I made my way back into the crowd and as I neared the courtyard, I saw a congregation forming. I approached from behind, eager to look over shoulders and see what the fuss was. The courtyard was full of sarcophaguses, patriarchs, and matriarchs of Oyotunji and priests delivering libations.

I was tapped on the shoulder and turned to see one of the men I had spoken with earlier. "We must speak with the king before the celebrations begin," he said solemnly and led me to another courtyard. There he was, dressed completely in white with many different colored scarfs draped around his shoulders. On his head sat a golden cloth Crown. Behold, Oba Adenfunmi II, the King of Oyotunji.

The man bowed at the waist and uttered a greeting I did not understand. Judging by the inflection it was obviously a gesture of respect. The King bowed half as deep as his subject had. He returned the greeting then adjusted his gaze to stare at me with copper eyes. I hadn't been briefed on what phrase was acceptable to use when greeting the king so I bowed quickly at the waist and introduced myself. I wasn't sure if it was permissible to touch him so I waited for him to respond. He extended his hand and I shook it somewhat relieved. He had been raised in the states and was content to greet me in a way that would set me at ease.

He smiled when I wished him happy birthday but that was when I realized that I had forgotten the basket in the car. It would have to wait because as I gave the king a brief synopsis of why I was there, he began walking me through the village and telling me about both his people and their ways.

We walked past strange stucco houses that I would learn are called a name that oddly translates into "*earth ships.*" The king explained that they were hurricane proof. It wasn't hard to believe. They were short structures with small arched doors you had to bend over to enter. No more than five feet tall, they looked like they were made from a single piece of stucco in the shape of large textured mushrooms with burgundy tops and white adornments.

On the other side of the small dirt street were large stucco deities. He showed me one of particular interest painted the color of the ocean, measuring at least twelve feet tall. It had a small concrete pool about six inches deep, ten feet long, and six feet wide. It reminded me of a water hazard at an aging putt-putt golf course in my hometown. This was the deity of the ocean, a matriarch to these people. My eyes wandered to an entire row of stucco deities lining the dirt road. We stopped at each and I was mesmerized by one that had a life sized voodoo dolls inside. It was a female doll, seated and leaning against the rough wall. From a distance, it looked like a real person sitting in the dark cave like dwelling.

I knew one trip would not be enough to take in all that was Oyotunji. I truly wanted to share this with others, if possible. We continued walking and a large iron bird sitting atop a perch outside one of the buildings grabbed my attention. It was made of old wood and covered in faded blue paint. It was easy to discern something different about this building, even among this forest of odd structures. "What is this building used for, your Highness?" I asked. The guide walking with us spoke for the king and said, "This room is where we go to contact ancestral spirits; this is where *we go to them.* You would call this the *astral projection* room." I was amazed he knew the term. These folks were not ignorant to outside ways but I felt extremely ignorant to theirs…astral projection, indeed.

The king said he was interested in having groups come to Oyotunji to see how the villagers live. He hoped it might clear up exaggerations and misunderstandings. I agreed with his contention but I knew the reality of Oyotunji would still be a shock to most outsiders. For example, animal sacrifice is indeed practiced but he was quick to add, everything sacrificed is consumed. To him it was no more evil than eating a chicken sandwich. In fact, it was more profound the animal died in ritual and was used as an offering to the deities and ancestors with nothing going to waste.

Then we spoke of *possession*. He did not attempt to hide the fact that possession is a very real part of their practice. He explained it was common for priests trained to become voluntarily possessed, to do so anytime they were attempting to gain knowledge or power in an endeavor. He spoke of bartering with the spirits using objects known to have been enjoyed by the patriarchs in life; commodities like rum, food or wine. During possession ceremonies, the priest can partake, giving the ancestor an opportunity to enjoy those things once again. In exchange, they offered guidance, protection and good fortune for the people of Oyotunji.

I must admit, hearing the king speak of possession and animal sacrifice made it seem almost mundane. I wasn't sure there was way for a white man like me to convey that message to a mostly white tour group. It might be hard to reconcile the same people who practiced willful possession and believed in the shedding of blood for favor; also offered words to live by and nothing to fear.

I accepted that some clients I might bring would have their own ways as well, which could seem strange to the people of Oyotunji. The mediums, the mystics, the folks who might be channeling energy from the Pleiades upon arrival...the paranormal investigators who would want to measure the various energies of this and that with numerous electronic instruments.

I envisioned the possibility of some glib, critical statement made by some halfwit who didn't take the time to read the tour description carefully and booked it anyway because it had a high ranking on a travel site. This is the Bible belt after all. Some people see these practices as outright sin and unavoidably one of them would end up with me, despite my best effort.

If I could find a way to appease both sides by presenting the story of Oyotunji with the marvel and wonderment it deserves, while at the same time, not overstep boundaries on either side; we would have one hell of a good tour on our hands. I was amazed and thrilled the king agreed. He knew there were risks on both sides and the planning would be tenuous. Beyond that though, we both felt it would foster understanding, if not acceptance.

The festivities were about to begin and my time with the king had expired. I told him I would be back to discuss further plans and he informed me I would return when the time was right. That was five long years but when the time came, not only would I meet Oyotunji's head voodoo priestess, but I would also witness spirit possession, firsthand.

Since finishing this book I have been granted permission to conduct tours at Oyotunji in collaboration with the priests and guides there. If you would like more information about these special night tours please visit blueorbtours.com death's MASQUERADE ✦

I've been to Oyotunji frequently since my first fateful visit. However, my appearance in February 2012 would bring my understanding of how influential Voodoo is in the low country full circle.

I had scheduled a meeting with King Oba Adegbolu Adenfunmi II. Beau Kester of Round1 Productions was along for the ride and he was prepared to document the interview portion of my meeting with the King and his Court. Neither of us knew what was in store.

When we arrived at Oyotunji, I saw familiar faces and just as before, all of the attendees were dressed in solid white. However, the atmosphere was completely different from my first visit. People recognized me from previous visits and had warmed to me to an extent. My nods were returned with their nods. The parking lot was packed and people swarmed the market square. It was obvious festival season had arrived.

There was some confusion when first checked in and we wondered if the interview would materialize. After quite a bit of back and forth, one of the King's attendants found us and said he would meet with us after the festival. I decided as long as we were there, we might as well get some footage. It would be useful for transitions once we edited the interview. Little did we know that what we were about to film would in many ways overshadow our interview with the King.

The festival we witnessed was the Egungun Masquerade and the people of Oyotunji were the first Orisha worshippers in the West to reinstitute it. We really had no idea the purpose of the festival but I felt a great anticipation in the air as we began setting up the cameras. The drummers were already in place and many people had gathered in a small set of bleachers in the main square. The king's court had assembled around his mobile throne but the king himself had not yet arrived. As we continued setting up, we both noticed the drumbeats had become more intense, more deliberate, and louder.

I went to the car to get my notebook. When I returned the king had taken his place on the makeshift throne. The drumming had magnified again and the Orisha devotees danced in the square. Many chanted as they twirled. The sound was beautiful although the meaning was a mystery to me. My attention shifted as a new character appeared in the square: The Egungun. This masquerader stood out in a long, brilliant, multicolored robe with a matching headpiece that prevented even his eyes from being exposed. We would find out later, the dance we were witnessing was in fact, the Death Masquerade. It is when all of the deceased matriarchs and patriarchs of Oyotunji, free from the sarcophagus were, now embodied in this single masquerader as one entity. To achieve this, the Egungun, along with the priests of Oyotunji, had performed a willful possession ceremony.

We watched the Egungun glide and twirl effortlessly amongst the crowd. Through interpretive symbolism, the Egungun was showing the villagers the amoral behavior that had occurred in the year since the last ceremony. It was the embodiment of all the love, power, knowledge and wisdom of these ancient peoples. The reckoning was being carried out in this penitence ceremony. Some of the people in the bleachers tapped their feet, hands were raised, and quite often, they would alternate between sitting down and re-joining the dance. Voices and drums filled the evening air and it became difficult to hear the people next to me talking. By this time, it seemed most everyone present was in a light trance or, at the very least, completely focused on the events unfolding. Our presence was irrelevant and unnoticed.

Finally, a fiery-eyed man dressed in tribal garb stepped from nowhere and escorted the Egungun over to another throne-like chair that had been placed to the right of the king. The Egungun sat in the chair, still moving rhythmically as people in the crowd drew near and dropped to their knees. There was a small basket for offerings and people deposited money, fruit, and handwritten notes. The Egungun sat in the chair for about 10 minutes accepting alms and shaking. The masquerader's escort then brought out a simple stick and laid it lengthwise between the king and the Egungun. Soon after, both rose from their seats and moved toward the other, but it was obvious they made every effort to stay on opposite sides of the stick boundary.

They faced one another and the king began hurling mysterious chants at the Egungun. I was later informed that the Egungun was also addressing the king; uttering prophecies, blessings and direction for the people in the coming year. No one ever saw the Egungun's face and it was much too loud for me to discern anything that was spoken. This spiritual exchange went on for almost 15 minutes when all at once, the crowd became very excited and celebratory. As the ceremony closed, the king returned to his throne, which was flanked by his mother and also the chief Voodoo priestess. The dancing continued for the better part of an hour and seemed effortless for everyone. No one was short of breath or appeared tired, despite the advanced age of some participants. The mystery deepened.

Although it had been a very mild winter, I noticed the temperature had dropped dramatically during the dance. I retrieved my wool coat and bottled water. I felt strange about what I had just witnessed. It had seemed almost ordinary while it was going on but when I considered we had just casually observed a willful possession, my mind started to spin. And if I believed this centuries old ritual, then I had not just observed a person possessed by a spirit, but a man possessed by *many* spirits.

In all honesty, save my surprise from the costume, the service resembled a full Gospel Christian church. It was a group of people celebrating, not a thing to be feared or exorcised. The willful possession had been joyful and would surely bring blessings. It caused me to confront my own beliefs and ponder the validity of the adage; the devil is usually simply the God of another people.

I was also informed of an exorcism of sorts. According to tradition, the Egungun masquerader released the spirits during an exit ceremony. We weren't allowed to see this occur, so I have no details as to how the act was accomplished. I felt sure it was a part of the tenets of the secret society, so out of respect I didn't inquire about it during the interview.

The festival moved into the nearby courtyard and quieted down. I watched the king stoically rise from his throne, along with this court, and begin the procession to the deepest part of Oyotunji. As outsiders, we needed an invitation to enter. It was a part of the village I had not been allowed to see before and it held the king's private quarters.

We are asked to remove our shoes before entering the king's home. It is simple, clean and orderly and propane heaters provided a radius of warmth. As I sat in a chair close to one of them, I began to lose some of the February chill that had arrived with the setting sun.

We weren't kept waiting long as the king and his court began flowing into the room. Several cameras were set up to record the interview and a young woman brought glasses of wine to those gathered in seats around the room.

I stood to greet the king who was jovial and talkative. He was more relaxed than he appeared at The Masquerade and it was apparent he felt satisfied with the Festival's success. After exchanging pleasantries and introductions, the interview began.

The king was seated on a different throne. This one was larger and although more primitive, it appeared more befitting a Voodoo king. It was a permanent fixture in the main room and sat on a stage of sorts and was higher than the surrounding floor where his advisors and his chief priestess were positioned.

The king nodded at me and it was my signal to begin asking my questions. "Thank you, your Highness for speaking with me today," began a most enlightening conversation. As we moved through our discussion, we explored the details I have provided above and throughout the chapters in this book. Of particular interest, were the words of the King's chief advisor and head Voodoo priestess at Oyotunji, Her Excellency Oloye Aina Olomo.

An educated woman with a long, wise face and large dark glasses; she was wearing the customary white attire, large glasses with blue lenses that are so common to see on an authentic conjurer and a matching blue necklace. Her Excellency had taught the concept of Voodoo at major accredited universities and she asked the King's permission to share a few words.

As she spoke on camera the precepts she wished to be taken back to the modern world, my world, one comment stuck with me. This is the summation:

"*Voodoo is no longer a fringe cult. It is one of the 8 religions that are shaping the world... and it is gaining more influence every day.*"

the BONE COLLECTORS ❧

"They's life in bones and its all we leave behind."
- ELSIE SHELOVE

The structure of modern western societies, combined with a well-equipped police force, has largely halted public digging for human remains. This prevents conjurers, Hoodoo practitioners, and Obeah priests from engaging in bone collection on the scale that was possible in times past, or on other shores.

However, even in the absence of willing witnesses, there are still the tell-tale signs and many people speak of it. I first heard of the practice occurring in the low country when speaking with Conjurers who reside just outside of Savannah's historic district. I was surprised to hear local residents who lived near secluded cemeteries tell stories of strange people in peculiar dress lurking among the tombstones late at night.

The motivation for human bone collecting is simple…occult magick. The bones of the dead are believed to hold power for the living. In the same way a bloodhound captures scent from pieces of clothing; conjurers wield the essence of the departed by harvesting their bones. They are the last remnant of the mortal coil.

In the low country, I've seen animal bones used to make musical instruments, works of art and of course, in ritual. The tossing and reading of them is a widely accepted fact. Most often, small animals like possums and chickens are used but there is also a great deal of evidence showing *human* bones are sought after for their strong occult power.

In some Conjuring societies, it is not unheard of for a person to leave their bones behind for use in rituals that would protect and bless the surviving loved ones. In our culture, it equates to leaving ashes behind after cremation. Willing the entire skeleton is no more shocking in 'conjuh'.

The skull is the most prized bone. In life, the skull contained the seat of the soul...the thought, will, intellect, and emotion of a person. It is easy to understand why the choicest bones for conjuring are *human* skulls and the bowls made from them are used for the highest forms of magick. The skull is renowned for its ability to evoke a spirit for an *in-person* house call. This ritual harnesses the residual energy of everything that makes us spiritual beings. The value is so powerful, their use can even be found in the history of Tibetan Buddhists who made cups from a 'kapala' (Sanskrit for skull).

In modern times, this practice brings up images of places like Jamaica, Mexico and Haiti. A recent news report from Spartanburg, South Carolina, however, validated my belief that it continues in the United States as well.

The article was released by Channel 5 KSDK on March 29, 2012. Just 250 miles from Savannah, grave robbers entered Oakwood Cemetery, also known as "Hell's Gate Cemetery"; a coffin was unearthed and the skull ritualistically taken. The burial grounds are iconic in the paranormal community for the unexplained mists, apparitions and supernatural anomalies witnessed when crossing through "Hell's Gate".

The ultimate purpose for taking it is anyone's guess; there are countless ways a skull could be used to interact with spirits. The rest of the skeleton, whether human or not, can also be used in a variety of ways. Collectors hang the bones in trees around planting fields, in order to bless the ground and guarantee a successful harvest. In ancient times, macabre scarecrows, made of entire skeletons, were mounted on sticks in the midst of the crops to ward off evil spirits and pestilence.

In present-day Savannah, you will find communities raising goats for use in ritual sacrifice. The animal is consumed at a feast, divided among the village's inhabitants and nothing is wasted...especially the bones. The skulls hang above the altars long after the flesh has been sacrificed. They are regarded as powerful tools for honoring and interacting with the dead.

There are carnal motivations for bone collecting as well. It is obviously an illegal vocation, and those willing to take the risk are rewarded with handsome sums of money and even esteem.

When I inquired about details of this practice in the low country, I found the stories weren't much different from what I had heard in the Caribbean. There were warnings, which urged me to keep a close eye out for hunters on bicycles late at night with a 5-gallon bucket hanging over the handlebars. A military shovel could usually be seen propped in the container and to those *in the know*, it was obvious they were seeking human bones.

My only encounter in Savannah with a possible *human* bone collector came one night while I was conducting a Midnight Zombie Tour. I was interrupted during my final story by a man who suddenly emerged from the bushes beside me. He was dressed in green shorts, a brown T-shirt and was holding a 5-gallon bucket and a small shovel. He attempted to slip away but an older woman in our group had already noticed him. As the rest of the crowd turned to look at the man, he seemed to sense it and looked back over his shoulder at us. His eyes appeared wild but calm. He dropped the shovel into the bucket and climbed onto a bicycle leaning against the wall of a home just across the street.

Soon after, I heard the ignition of a vehicle with a noisy exhaust system a little further down the street. We watched a plain white van avoid using its lights as it made an immediate left turn, heading north out of the historic district. The event shocked everyone, including me. No one in the crowd even joked we might have paid an actor to put on a show. In fact, the subject matter we discussed that night had nothing to do with bone collecting. Quite honestly, I don't know if anyone on the tour even realized what he might be doing. I decided to keep quiet about my suspicions but afterward I walked back to the bushes where the man had emerged, and cautiously ventured in.

I discovered a freshly dug hole about three feet deep and roughly the diameter of a small dinner plate. There were exposed roots and obvious signs the shovel had cut into them. Some appeared to have been manually snapped, indicating he resorted to using his hands...perhaps just about the time 20 people on a ghost tour ventured into a part of Savannah where tours don't usually go at that late hour.

My belief the man had been digging for remains was reinforced by the fact we encountered him in a city square that sits atop a well-known but unmarked slave cemetery. Utility workers unwittingly exhumed human remains buried below, including a skull, while attempting to install a meter, and local newspapers publicized the finding.

We have since discontinued the Midnight Zombie Tour and resurrected it in the form of the Uncensored Zombie Tour. It currently starts at 10 p.m. rather than midnight. I haven't seen anything comparable since that night. I'm not sure, it may have been an anomaly, or perhaps we happened to be at the right place at the right time.

I am still in those places, though at different hours. I do occasionally see the undeniable figure, riding a bicycle with the telltale bucket on the handlebars. I look at his hands and knees. Are they dirty? His shorts stained? His bucket full? Even if we don't exchange glances I find it impossible not to wonder where he is going.

ELSIE ✦

I had been speaking with Hoodoo and Conjuh' practitioners in and around Savannah but as my questions grew more specific about their local practices, they recognized my hunger for a deeper understanding of the low country variety of Hoodoo culture. At that point, I was told I would need to speak with Elsie Shelove.

Finding her was no easy task. Many suggestions led nowhere and Elsie was apparently an alias. I was finally introduced to a woman named Nicole, who claimed to be her niece. She was in her early twenties...tall, lean and very attractive with a quiet look in her eyes that seemed older than her years. "I can try to introduce you to Elsie but I cannot promise she will speak with you."

I gave Nicole my number and asked her to call me as soon as she heard something. I was surprised when I received the good news just a few hours later. "She will meet with you." I arranged to meet Nicole the next day at a small roadside market just outside of Savannah. She would take me to Elsie from there. Secretly, I was relieved she wanted to meet in a public place.

The following day I drove to the market. I left early to give myself plenty of time but when I pulled into the lot, to my surprise, Nicole was already there. She was leaning on her car and texting from a small pink phone. "Follow me. It is about 20 minutes from here." I wondered why Nicole had been willing to help me and why Elsie had so readily agreed. If it was a setup, it was too late to care.

The "twenty minutes" turned into half an hour and we had been on roads I was unfamiliar with for the better half of the journey. Narrow two-lanes gave way to a dirt road for about 2 miles. Finally, we pulled into the large yard of a grey shuddered house that looked dim and quiet. A medium sized white dog of no particular breed barked and followed as we slowly pulled alongside the house and parked. There were no other cars in the yard and I wondered if Elsie was really there.

"Wait here," Nicole said softly as she confidently made her way up the uneven block steps and pulled open the screen door without knocking. I waited against my car and tried to appease the still nagging dog. Nicole reappeared at the door and gave a quick wave, signaling me to enter.

I stepped on the porch and immediately the age and deterioration of the house became apparent. The screen door was frail and seemed mostly decorative. The house smelled like rotting wood and there was a quilt hanging on the back of an old green recliner. Surrounding a cloth sofa were hand built end tables, both covered with curious items...small copper colored bells next to an ashtray full of spent hand rolled cigarettes on one table; marbles in a yellow glass bowl surrounded by small candles on the other. A weathered portrait of a black Jesus hung above a surprisingly modern television.

Nicole walked through the living room into the kitchen and exited onto the back porch through another screen door. The door hung open on its own and I could hear Nicole was talking to someone who was still out of my sight. I followed along making my way gingerly onto the back porch. At last, here was Elsie.

She was a large woman wearing a simple white dress. Dirty pink house slippers covered her feet and she had short-cropped hair sprinkled with gray. She wore a woven necklace with a small wooden charm and many tarnished bracelets around her wrists and forearm, the higher ones squeezing her skin between them. She had a silver metal ring on each hand with a single, small faded stone.

"Pull up dat chair, hear?" Elsie said as she motioned her hand quickly to the thin wooden chair at the opposite end of the porch. I walked over to grab it and place it diagonal to her chair, which was fitted with a large mismatched cushion. "It's a pleasure to meet you Ms. Shelove." She nodded her head as she shelled field peas into a large blue plastic bowl. "What bring you here to me today?" I had to consider my answer, realizing I didn't know specifically why I was here, only that I felt I needed to be. "I feel I am supposed to meet you." It was the most honest answer I could muster, odd as it sounded leaving my mouth. "Well, let's go inside and see why you here." She laid the shelled peas on the unfinished ones waiting in a black metal 5-gallon bucket.

Elsie reached for a cane leaned next to her and I understood why there was no other car in the yard. Her ankles were swollen and misshapen. It was one of the worst cases of arthritis I had ever seen. I was amazed at how effortlessly she raised her frame on such worn joints. She rocked to the side as she walked and turned sideways to go through the half opened screen door. We made our way back to the living room and I was careful not to walk too closely behind her as she shuffled toward the recliner.

She pushed back the recliner in one fluid motion and it locked loudly into place as she put her feet up to rest. "Reach me my tray, 'Cole baby." Nicole slid her hand under the sofa and brought out a bronze colored serving tray. Elsie took the tray and laid it across her lap. There was a small pipe half-full of tobacco, a small box of matches and a small burlap bag. "Light me those candles," she said to Nicole as she handed her the matches from the tray. She attended to them quickly and quietly.

There were no lights on in the house, and even with two screen doors and a cloudless sky outside, the living room felt unusually dark. The candles began to dance shadows on the rustic walls and Elsie sat stoically for a few moments before she methodically picked up the small bag from the tray. "Ok, they here now. Be still." I had heard this before in ceremonies in Haiti so I knew she meant *the spirits*.

Elsie began to hum as she worked the sack with her hands. A few minutes went by and the humming grew faint as she looked down into her lap. I wasn't sure if she was falling asleep or going into a trance. Before I could decide, she slowly tipped the bag downward and tiny bones began tinkling and tumbling onto the tray and then settled. I felt tightness in my neck as I watched her run her hands over them. She wasted no time interpreting the signs.

"UmmHmm…this a strange one…UmmHmm…sho' is." Elsie continued studying the small prickly bones. As I looked closer at the tray and the bones, I noticed one of them was broken. The layout was a

mystery to me but to Elsie, they grabbed her attention as if she was watching a fascinating but coherent story unfold. The intensity of her focus pulled me in and I found myself shifting from keen curiosity to swelling anticipation.

"The Hag have a sight on you. They know you here....UmmHmm...." Elsie continued to pause and stare.

"You gonna need a stone." Elsie stared at me stoically and left her gaze resting on me as if gauging my level of understanding as to what she was saying. "A stone?" I asked. Elsie looked away and stared back at the bones as quickly as my question. The probing gaze had been a formality for her. The predictability of my ignorance turned her back to the mystery of the bone pile. "People do they best to stay clear of the Hag 'round here. Why you doin' yo best to get on one?" Elsie leaned back in the recliner as she asked me and stared at the ceiling. Quickly dissatisfied, she took no comfort in the exposed beams and began staring at the black Jesus hanging above the television instead. It was apparent she was quite bothered.

"I guess I am confused Ms. Elsie, I don't feel like I am trying to *get up on a Hag*." My throat felt like it melted together as I uttered that name but it was the most assertive thing I had said since arriving. Elsie, undaunted, became more agitated. "Boy they been following you a while now....or maybe you been followin' them?" She acted as if she'd been too familiar with me in her statement and now thought it proper to look straight ahead at no particular point. She reached for the arm to let out the recliner. When she realized it was already fully extended, she quickly put her hands back in her lap and tapped her thighs quickly several times as if frustrated with her nervous gesture.

The atmosphere in the room grew tense. I had forgotten Nicole until she came gingerly back into the frame, moving behind Elsie, putting several fingertips on her aunt's shoulder and gently leaning on the recliner. Elsie reached back and patted the top of Nicole's hand, acknowledging the comfort.

I felt obligated to break the hanging silence and change Elsie's appraisal of me but no words would form. I sat there waiting for what seemed like a verdict. Elsie stared on, waiting for what seemed like direction.

"I'm goin' to give you two things." Elsie closed the recliner purposefully, her weight caused it to shift and stall before she gave it a quick push with her heel. She paused before standing, careful not to tip the tray of bones. It also afforded her a moment to prepare her ankles to bear the weight of her frame. Nicole offered her hands, one for Elsie the other for the tray.

Elsie walked hunched over toward the kitchen. I sat and watched Nicole carefully slide the tray under the sofa and back to its resting place. I noticed she did not touch the bones or the small bag that had contained them. I heard the pantry door open and saw Elsie's shadow pause. She began to effortlessly hum a familiar tune. Most conjurers I had met hummed while practicing their craft as if each one had a special frequency at which they liked to work. The sound comforted me and the tension in the room seemed to acquiesce to the melody and readily slipped away.

Elsie hobbled back into the room. Invigorated and absorbed by her work, she wasn't using the cane that had been so necessary only minutes before. "You take this, its fo' protection." She dropped a small stone in my hand with a rough natural doughnut hole in its center. "Use a string to keep it held around you. Make sho' it's a plant string. Wit dis' you kin see a Hag and it'll protect you from em'." I rolled the odd stone around in my hand slowly, curious as to where this could have been found naturally in the low country. "An' take these. Burn em' like I tell ya and say what I tell ya when you do. It'll get all evil people away from you and all the mess they tryin' to bring and protect you from it comin back." Elsie handed me three black, hand pressed candles rolled in burlap. They were rough and dark, about 4 inches long. They felt substantial. Powerful, even.

"When you git home take a salt bath. When you git out the bath don't dry off with no towel. Don't put on no clothes, just go sit in the dark and light one candle….use a sulphur match. Sit in that room and let that candle burn til it go out. If it go out don't light it again, now. While it's burnin' and you sittin' jus be still. You'll start seein' all kinds of mess, people tryin' to bring on you. When you see it, you tell it to go. You say it and mean it now, Go! Once you done that, it'll leave out and go back on the person tryin' to bring it on ya. You do that 3 nights and it'll be gone. Don't wait till the moon starts gettin' full again, do it now while it's goin' away and it'll take all the mess away with it." I paused to take it all in. I didn't know if I would do what she was asking but I was intent on hearing her out. "What about the stone?" I asked.

"The stone is for wearin'. Do it like I said. Wear it much as you can, 'specially at night. 'Specially when you sleep. You have to wear it a while to start seein' a Hag but it'll protect you from 'em right from tha start. Ain't but one thing at a time can be put in it and that one is for protection. It been buried at a crossroads."

Part of me wanted to call bullshit. There was no way this woman without a car and debilitating arthritis had made it down to a crossroads and buried this stone. On the other hand, she was troubling herself to make hand pressed candles, readily knew what moon phase we were in and her reputation was unquestioned by those that knew her. I had also seen the energy she invoked while at work, how she had glided effortlessly though the kitchen. I had seen conjurers in Haiti and Jamaica go to incredible lengths to empower objects. So, just like in those places, I was left with "What if?"

I backed away from my original inclination but I still had a burning question I couldn't take with me. "Thank you, Ms. Elsie. I really appreciate it. "May I ask you something?" I ventured. "How is it you saw this from the bones? And the Hag? Why me? Or is it everyone?" I wondered if I was the one acting too familiar this time but if I was going to be placed in the role of patient/client, I thought it reasonable to ask questions.

"Mos ery'one come up on a Hag at some point. ' Specially round here. Mos times people suffer from em' and don't know what to call em'. You been round a lot a places to get in one and you goin' to more. You need protectin' sure as I'm standin' here." I found her comment resonated with me, no matter how critical I tried to be.

"What about the chicken bones, Ms. Elise? How did you see that from using chicken bones?" "They's possum bones, not chicken," she quickly responded. "Possums see at night so they can know what's hidden. They good for seein' lies and gettin' direction. Possums good for scryin' on things. They's life in bones and it's all we leave behind."

I sat in solemn silence as I tried to find a suitable way to transition the conversation. "What may I give you for your time and trouble, Ms.

Elsie?" She looked at me gently. It was the first sign of softness I had seen from her. "You have to decide that yo' self." That was a new one! I had never spoken with a conjurer that didn't have a fixed price or at least, recommend a return visit. Elsie shied from both. I pulled out some money and gave her what I hoped would be expected.

She took it and folded her fist around it. "You take care and don't be takin no chances." I put my hand on her shoulder and smiled. Conjurers are careful about touching and I had done it without thinking but it had seemed natural and she didn't seem to mind. "May I visit you again, Ms. Elsie?" She looked down and smiled, "If you need me again jus talk to Cole' and we'll see what we be needin' to do."

Again, I had forgotten about Nicole. "Do you remember how to get back?" she asked. "Yeah, I think I can manage. Thank you for helping me." She nodded as I gently opened the frail door and made my way down the stairs of the old porch where the dog peeked one lazy eye at me and returned to his sleep. One back leg was slowly kicking and I concluded the rabbit or car he was chasing in his dream was offering more sport than I promised.

Once I had gotten back on roads I recognized, I reflected on my meeting with Elsie. I began to see her in a kinder light. Hell, she'd gone to the trouble to get possum bones and was quick to tell me the difference. It mattered to her.

And there were specific things she knew about me. Yes, at this point, I considered *Hags* to be specific things about me given my experience in Savannah but I also knew Hag stories were plentiful here. The bottom line for me, I felt Elsie was as real as real could be, if you believe in the power of a conjurer. Maybe Elsie had actually made her way down to a crossroad. Maybe everything she said was true. My mouth went dry and I took a sip of water as I adjusted the stone and candles in my pocket.

The sun was setting as I began the 2-mile trek across Talmadge Bridge. Two hundred feet below, the shoreline was beginning to flicker with activity and the Savannah River caught rays of warm, setting sunlight. They lay gently on the water, moving in rhythm with the small waves. The glow of Savannah and the soft murmur of the river below calmed my thoughts.

As the Historic District took me in, I was reminded of the epitaph of poet Conrad Aiken, who is buried in Bonaventure, the famous Victorian era cemetery just outside of Savannah. I conduct tours of Bonaventure and I always tell my guests the story of how Aiken once watched a ship head out to sea. It was named The *Cosmos Mariner.* Destination - Unknown. The words had made such an impact on him that he had it inscribed on his gravestone.

In that moment, I felt I understood exactly how he must have identified with that very mysterious ship.

don't LOOK, *don't* RUN ✦

*Take a black cat bone and a guitar and go to a lonely fork in
the roads at midnight. Sit down there and play your best piece,
thinking of and wishing for the devil all the while.
By and by you will hear music, dim at first but growing
louder and louder as the music approaches.*
(FROM BELIEFS OF THE SOUTHERN NEGRO BY NEWBELL NILES PUCKETT)

I explored Savannah and the outlying area for spells and practices that were as close to universally accepted as I could find. Repeatedly, I was led to the power of the *crossroads*. Everyone that wanted to perform high magick said they had gone to the crossroads to do it properly, but I became fixated on what happens once you *came* to the crossroads.

The crossroads are the international waters of the spirit world, an organic makeshift altar where free from influence and arbiters, a person can come face-to-face, unencumbered with the other side. The inherent value seems to be, when you stand there, you are neither here *nor* there.

It is also a safe place to dispose of used magical items that have been employed in previous rituals. Buried in the ground, there is no worry that some unsuspecting passerby will become spiritually entangled by another conjurers magic.

The crossroads also seems to serve as a meeting place where you can chance upon what is sometimes referred to as *"The Dark Man"* or some other powerful spiritual entity. The encounter promises unrivaled gain and skill to benefit you in this life. It could be a talent for gambling, magick or playing a musical instrument. The possibilities really are endless; you need only know how to carry out the ritual correctly.

In my own visits to the Georgia Guidestones outside of Elberton, I learned that the Cherokee Indians view that area as a spiritual crossroads; a prime location for practicing magick.

Years later, a man named R.C. Christian (a pseudonym) must have realized it as well. The story goes, he walked into an Elberton bank just a few miles from the crossroads and laid out the plans for a set of guide stones to be erected. A time capsule entombed in a granite vault would be buried next to them. The contents would lend direction to what was left of mankind after the impending worldwide disaster that he, and the group he represented, believed was imminent. Elberton's large granite deposits are the foundation upon which it sits. They would be impenetrable to a nuclear exchange or a worldwide disaster in the mind of R.C. Christian and it would make a perfect environment to erect the Guidestones.

In historic Savannah, I have noticed the squares all form a crossroad of sorts; east-west roads intersecting north-south roads. I've often wondered if that part of their design was intentional…for mystical reasons and not just city engineering. Perhaps, that's why so many of the squares in Savannah lend themselves to hauntings and are fertile fields for paranormal anomaly.

Of all the different rituals I encountered involving the crossroads, there seem to be none so powerful or as widely recognized as *Cross Bones*. The ceremony is so highly regarded; it seems to be the Colonial "Bloody Mary" ritual for conjuring folk who are determined to come face to face with the other side.

What I heard firsthand from those who had tried it, almost without exception, was it produced the desired effect and it was not intended for the faint of heart or upstarts. You see, the ritual is regarded as fail-proof, but only if you *don't look* and *don't run*.

Incidentally, those that failed admitted it was because of fear. Once begun, the most important rule to heed…do not run, or look at *The Blackness* as it approaches. The unsuccessful had lost their courage and fled. To avoid this, continue practicing your chosen talent under the waxing moon. In various cases, The *Blackness* came as a man, a mist, a cat or even a simple shadow.

We also learned in some instances, it did not take a full waxing cycle to get the intended result; however, it always appeared by the time the full moon arrived.

The most advantageous method promoted a natural intersection of paths in a field or the woods. Another favorable route was to travel by foot to a crossroad, formed by intersecting dirt roads.

We interviewed a gentleman regarded as having successfully completed *Cross Bones*. The practical application breaks down to this:

Take two bones (I'm going to refrain from revealing what type of bone was used) and cross them in the middle of the crossroads. Begin to practice your craft right before midnight on the first night of a waxing moon.

You must bring whatever skill you wish to learn with you and the more specific you can be, the better. For example, if you want to be a world-class gambler, what game is your poison? Blackjack? Bring a deck. Dice? Let 'em roll. Get the idea?

As the one you seek to meet draws near, you will see subtle changes. The sightings are distinct because deities take different forms and major in all manner of trades.

The man we questioned chose to become adept at speaking and swaying others with his words. Standing at the crossroads before midnight, he began saying whatever filled his heart. He would continue until his capacity for speaking was exhausted and quietly return home, never looking back.

This went on for seven or eight nights (He contradicted himself by saying "seven" in one interview and "eight" during the subsequent interview), before things started to change. The first transformation he distinguished was the owls began congregating to hear his words. Then frogs. Pretty soon, the crickets stopped to hear him talk. And then the shadows came.

He said he noticed them as the moon started becoming brighter on his last visits. They were easier to see in the moonlight and he watched them in the tree line, waiting and listening. Finally, he said, a large dark shadow walked out of the tree line and he could feel it towering behind him. He didn't turn or run, even though everything inside of him screamed it was the right thing to do. He just kept speaking.

His mouth was open when an icy cold form came into his body and his knees went weak. He was still speaking but the words were not his own. He felt his stomach begin to cramp and his eyes welled. He kept pushing sounds out of his mouth.

Finally, the cramps in his stomach became unbearable and he was sure he was going to vomit. And vomit he did. But not in a way he ever had before. What came out of his mouth was *honey*. The best he had ever tasted…just as if it had never been in his stomach. He said he hadn't eaten honey in years because of his "blood sugar", but here it was flowing out of him.

He finally had to stop speaking when his throat became full. He leaned forward to expel the substance from his mouth for the better part of an hour. Once he was finished, he sat there wiping the tears from his irritated eyes and the honey vomit from his face and neck.

He walked home slowly and said he'd never heard the woods so silent. He arrived home starving, ate six scrambled eggs and drank a glass of buttermilk. It was two days before the taste of honey was out of his mouth but since then he said, "I can talk a person into anything. I set a pitch and the persuasion just comes. All I have to do is put my mind to it and the words take care of themselves. A man, one time, gave me his beautiful hand carved cane because I took a few minutes to talk him into it."

So…did it really happen? Did it truly work? I'll never know. However, he told us this story exceptionally well. After all, it was one of dozens we choose to put in the book. In addition, I might mention, the walking cane that lay across his lap was a damn fine one.

shango's WIND ✒

My videographer and I were graced with a cloudless, perfect spring day in the Savannah low country. The kind of day so prized, when you looked back on a lifetime of spring days, you were able to remember every one like this. That's the day we witnessed what conjurers refer to as *Shango's Wind*.

Beau and I had purposely arrived late in the afternoon because, as any good photographer will tell you, dusk is the best light of the day. As we pulled into Oyotunji, we heard the familiar sound of loud drums. They were not coming from a tribal ceremony, but rather the speakers and sound system capable of pumping music throughout the settlement during festivals. There was no occasion this day; the music was playing to cadence the work of village residents who were preparing for a celebration occurring the following week.

Weary from a day of shooting at the 1790 Inn and the more than 50-mile drive to the settlement, we both had an immediate need for the restroom. As I walked in that direction, I noticed wooden barriers, the kind used to keep a crowd in check during a parade, formed a circle. Hanging on one of the barriers was a sign that read *Warning: Beehive Area*. In the middle, I saw a large fallen tree trunk with a gaping hole filled with bees. Instantly, I became aware of hundreds more flying around the hive. The lesson to remember any time you visit Oyotunji, never take a careless step here, literally or metaphorically.

The mild trauma of realizing I had almost walked into thousands of bees, combined with the primitive restroom facilities, resigned me to wait. I turned and made my own beeline to the center of the courtyard. I didn't see anyone but I noticed several cars parked at the southern end of the settlement. Beau was unpacking his camera equipment as I walked toward the cars. As I got closer, I noticed several men sitting on the beams of a skeletal foundation that would soon be a floor.

There were three men sitting and one man working. The man closest to me was smoking a small cigar and nodded his head when I said hello. One of the men, a chief, recognized me from a previous visit. We exchanged greetings, I explained I had spoken with the King and we were here to take photographs for the book. The chief asked me to wait, and sent one of the seated men to the king's private quarters at the northern end of the settlement.

I had waited on the king several times before and I knew it could be anywhere from a few minutes to a few hours. Beau had assembled all of his gear and he was anxious to begin the shoot. The strong shadows formed by the setting sun choose for us, as some of our subjects rested comfortably in shade, while others were still fully exposed beneath the cloudless sky.

We walked into a small inner courtyard, behind the hurricane-proof stucco dwellings that they refer to as *"earth ships"*. In front of us was a small altar overflowing with colored glass, fruit, jewelry and trinkets, plates, coins, incense and wooden carvings. Hanging above the altar from a triple braided cord, were the small skulls of baby goats and a bird, its beak still intact.

It was a beautifully morbid sight. We weren't entirely sure if we were supposed to be photographing this part of the settlement, so Beau immediately set up his equipment and began taking photos, (it's easier to get forgiveness than permission, right?).

As Beau finished shooting, I walked over to the stucco oddities and peered into the shadowy cave one of the dwellings. I was drawn to the full size voodoo doll, which sat with drawn-on eyes staring back at me from the dark innards of its permanent home. As I moved closer, I realized the entire doll was stuffed with Spanish moss. I contemplated the massive effort it must have been to gather that much moss. It reinforced yet another lesson to keep in mind while at Oyotunji; everything is authentic. I asked Beau to get a few shots of the massive voodoo doll and without looking up he said, "Already got it."

Back in the main area, a guide known simply as Bah-Bah greeted us. He explained he would assist us in our efforts. I asked him to take us to the courtyard of the priests where the two main temples sat, along with the tombs of Oyotunji's founders.

As we made our way to the courtyard, the king's mother arrived to greet me. I had spoken with her a few weeks earlier so I knew one of the temples under construction had been damaged by a bad storm. I had offered to donate to the rebuilding effort upon my next visit and she had graciously accepted. We spoke for a few minutes and she promised she would re-join us after she attended to some business at the king's quarters.

We continued into the priests' courtyard and I asked Beau to take a photo of the tomb of one of the founders. Beau decided he needed a small ladder to frame the photo properly and our guide informed us he would get one. We contemplated a list of our shots while we waited. Another man came into the courtyard to take my donation for the temple project and as I turned back to Beau, I saw Bah-Bah coming into the courtyard, ladder in hand.

I pointed to the Shango temple's altar and asked Bah-Bah if it was permissible to photograph the interior. Suddenly, an Oyotunji's resident, one I'd never seen, informed me the king's mother would like to see me. She stepped out of her quarters and embraced me with a kind and genuine hug. She thanked me for the donation and led me to the temple it was helping re-build. We made our way to a smaller construction, compared to the two main ones; it was the damaged temple.

The king's mother took me to the entrance and I customarily removed my shoes. There was already a shrine in place at the front of the temple and she picked up a sounding bell. She shook it quickly and in a jubilant voice began to speak things I could not understand. I assume it was Yoruba dialect, sprinkled in the midst of which, I heard my name. She then translated in English, telling the Voodoo deity I have given money for the construction of the temple. She asked for blessings and wished prosperity on me. I stood politely, unsure if anything was required on my part.

Back outside, she pointed to the roof section my funds would be used to complete. We embraced again and I made my way back to the priest's courtyard and the Shango Temple. The large doors of the temple were open and resting against the walls on either side of them.

Shango's colors are red and white and everything inside the temple adhered to that. He is the God of wind, lightning and thunder, a central deity in the voodoo belief system; most appropriately compared to Zeus in Greek mythology or the Father in the Christian Trinity. Beau and I wanted a clear shot of the temples interior but two white curtains obscured our view. With no wind in sight we decided we might have to pin them to the sides of the door. We had to make a decision quickly or abandon the shot. I was aware Bah-Bah was becoming restless after working in the heat all day. He made several polite but pointed comments about dinner waiting at home and I knew we were almost out of time.

I looked at Beau and said, "Maybe we'll get some wind so we don't have to pin back the curtains." Instantly, a strong rushing wind poured over the walls of the priest's courtyard. It was so strong it could be heard and I felt it approaching from behind. It washed over my shoulders like waves and kicked up a small cyclone of sand near us.

The curtains were indented slightly from the doorframe and it took a few moments for the wind to work its magic on them. When it did, they parted perfectly, gently rolling back, allowing Beau to get the perfect shot. By this time, we had been outside for several hours with no wind remotely this strong. As Beau finished the shot, there was one final burst of wind and the large ten-foot doors leading into the courtyard slammed shut.

The look on Beau's face said what I was feeling...what we all were feeling. Bah-Ba kissed two fingers and pointing at the sky said, "Shango gave this to us." Bah-Bah began praising Shango while Beau and I stared in disbelief.

Winds strong enough to move thin curtains are one thing, but a rushing wind, seemingly on cue, strong enough to close ten-foot doors is quite another. I immediately thought back to the blessing the King's mother requested for me and wondered if Shango's wind had spoken.

A sleek, coal black cat emerged from the tree line and joined us. There wasn't an ounce of surprise in me when Bah-Bah looked at the cat and said, "Where did you come from Lightning?" Beau and I both smiled. "Are you serious?" I asked. Bah-Bah looked at me curiously. "The cat, the cat's name is *Lightning*?" I said excitedly. "Oh, yes. We thought he was gone," Bah-Bah explained. "So let me get this straight; we just experienced an on-demand wind which made a sandy cyclone slam a ten foot gate shut, but it only made enough fuss over the curtains to peel them back perfectly for our photo? Followed by the triumphant return of an M.I.A. cat named *Lightning*...as we stand in front of the temple for the god of *wind* and *lightning*?" Bah-Bah laughed genuinely for several seconds and said simply, "Shango give us this wind." Indeed I grinned, and a little 'lightning' too.

A photo of Shango's temple and the mysterious kitty, 'Lighting', are included in this book. Additional photos available at Blueorbtours.com

SECTION THREE ✦ *Colonial Tales*

The Colonial version of ghost, spirits and all things strange is the one you are probably familiar with and the one you will hear espoused in Savannah.

The Colonial crowd has a very structured belief system. It is inversely proportionate to the Conjurers version in many ways; it is largely monotheistic, the day of death is mourned and the birthday celebrated. Its history has been meticulously recorded with well-established theories, and it continues to see the after-life as a place of reward or punishment. Human spirits staying behind are seen as lost and unable to move on or transition. Non-human spirits, if not angelic, are usually considered negative in nature. Possession is commonly against a persons will and because of some great immorality. Any deliberate attempt to contact spirits is frowned upon and any contact not made with heaven itself, at least to some, is outright sin. Most non-religious dealings with the after-life are approached scientifically, in the form of paranormal investigations. Contact with the other side is considered infrequent and seems to be treated with almost impenetrable skepticism.

This section begins with a series of events that are widely believed to have been the catalyst for the enormous amount of paranormal phenomena experienced in Savannah. It then moves straightforward into the eerie and mysterious occurrences reported here.

CITY *of the* DEAD ❧

There is little debate among Savannah residents; they live in America's most haunted city and there is one unifying reason. Savannah is built on its dead.

There are as many as seven partial cemeteries under Savannah's 2.2 square mile historic district. The total number of bodies is anyone's guess. The estimates range from inconsequential to over ten thousand.

I dismiss anyone who will attest to the exact number of souls or cemeteries under our streets but we can be sure of these:

❧ Parts of Colonial Park Cemetery interred at least 11,000 of Savannah's citizens from 1750 until 1853.

❧ A slave burial ground exists in the Calhoun square area, said to be the largest un-exhumed cemetery of the eighteenth century.

❧ There are numerous illegal burial sites preserved in and around Old Candler hospital.

Understanding the relationship the city has with the residents under its sidewalks is complex. However, it appears living atop so many of its former citizenry has created a dysfunctional connection between *us* and *them*. The fractured relationship was set in motion during Savannah's earliest childhood, when the living played the role of absent parents to the latchkey dead.

Adding fuel to the paranormal fire are the ways in which death came. They are mostly tragic, mostly untimely and mostly horrific in nature.

WAR

Besides innumerable skirmishes, the two greatest wars fought on U.S. soil were fought in and/or around Savannah. Predictably, the city has buried a great many casualties of war; most notably, those mortally wounded during the *Siege of Savannah*. This battle saw the bloodiest hour of the Revolutionary War and the second most deadly conflict of the entire war. American and British soldiers, enemies in life, now lay in eternal rest, side by side.

YELLOW FEVER

"All I desire for my own burial is not to be buried alive."
- Lord Chesterfield, 1769.

Yellow fever arrived in deadly waves as improvements in sea travel allowed the vector for spreading the epidemic to survive long enough to reach Savannah's shore. The subtropical climate, combined with large amounts of standing water from frequent spring rains made ideal breeding grounds for the virus-carrying mosquito.

According to The Georgia Historical Society, the first major epidemic struck in 1820 and had sinister undertones, claiming 666 victims. Many say the ominous symbolism of the number, prevented Savannah from putting the exact tally of victims on the memorial marker located in Colonial Park Cemetery. Instead, it commemorates an *estimate* of the dead as "...*nearly 700*".

It was a dark warning of things to come. Savannah was ravaged at least three more times from major yellow fever outbreaks and thousands more lives were claimed.

Contracting yellow fever was alarming was but there were more horrific possibilities which made the epidemic so feared. Chief among them was *not dying* and suffering the unimaginable possibility of a live burial. It was a very real fear for hundreds of years in America and yellow fever offered one of the best opportunities to be prematurely laid to rest.

You can hear tales of these live burials; stories of scratch, claw and bite marks found underneath coffin lids unearthed during expansion, or the habit of tying bells to thin ropes that were positioned in the hands of those placed in the coffin. In the event a person was buried alive, they could pull the rope from inside the casket; alerting anyone within earshot and offering hope to be "saved by the bell".

Those saved by the bell appeared yellow and gaunt after returning from the grave. In Savannah they were referred to as "the dead ringers". Today the term "dead ringer" is defined as an exact replica of an original. Many believed the survivors to be copies; soulless versions of the loved one they had laid to rest…the walking dead… zombies if you prefer.

Fear gripped the town and myths about how the fever was transmitted ran wild. Unfortunately, it would not be until the turn of the century that mosquitos would be identified as the cause.

In the meantime, cannons were fired down Bay Street in bizarre attempts to kill whatever was in the air causing the sickness. Fires were set ablaze in strategic locations to ward off the unknown cause and curfews were imposed to keep the population from panicking or fleeing the city by night. People were ordered indoors while mass burials were ghoulishly carried out under the cover of darkness.

This presented a curious problem because a late term symptom of yellow fever is a coma-like sleep. As the sickness continued to claim victims, the doctors and competent caregivers were among them. At that point, untrained volunteers were employed to help care for the sick and dying. Without modern medicine, hasty night burials and the ill-equipped overseeing the panic, many people in fever-induced comas were prematurely pronounced dead. It isn't hard to imagine what came next, even if it seems impossible to imagine what it must have been like.

The doomed soul would wake in the small coffin, claustrophobically pinned in the supine position. The air would have been stale, hot and pitch black. As the body continued to wake from the coma, oxygen consumption would resume at a near normal rate and slow suffocation would begin.

The victim would surely be drowsy and nauseous. Even uncrossing their arms in the blackness would have proved challenging in such a tight space. Attempts to push the immovable weight would have been futile. The desperation of clawing and scratching into the lid of the coffin would cause nausea to worsen. Likely, they would begin to vomit the oxidized blood in their stomach, which would now resemble coffee grounds. Unable to sit up, they would likely choke to death on the *black vomit,* as it was known, before having the opportunity to run out of air.

The fear of live burial followed us into modern times and patent filings show us safety coffins were designed to avoid being buried alive even as late as the 1980's. According to the United States Patents Office, one such device was called, "The *Improved Burial Case"* (Patent No. 81,437 Franz Vester, Newark, New Jersey. August 25, 1868.) The coffin came complete with a ladder, rope and bell...just in case.

STRANGERS

The hardest numbers of tragic deaths to estimate are the ones Savannah simply refers to as *"strangers".*

Early Savannah was small, concentric and built to be easily defended because of the military mission assigned it (Guarding South Carolina from the Spanish threat in Florida).

Immigrant populations and slave ships pulled into port weary and sick from long term ocean voyages. Those that died during the journey, or shortly after, were buried in the outlying woods while their family and loved ones moved on to settle in other places.

The dead were left behind in makeshift graves throughout what would later become greater Savannah. They were soon hard to distinguish, since no one was left to tend the site or memorialize its location. The innumerable unmarked graves stand in stark contrast to the formal places of rest, and eventually most of them were lost to development and forgotten.

Bone and coffin fragments from this time in the city's history are undeniably present. Slave remains were discovered even in this century as utility workers attempted to install a new meter on the edge of Calhoun Square.

Not far away, line workers found partial skeletons in the branches of a live oak. In all probability, these were victims of one of Savannah's devastating floods over a hundred years ago. We know that Hurricane Katrina victims are still being found in the trees of New Orleans. If Savannah is any predictor, they will continue to be for many years, if not centuries, to come.

It is reasonable to wonder why so many of the departed were simply built over rather than reinterred. Some *were* relocated but many were unable to afford the process, while countless others were lost to rapid development.

Expansion came, in part, after the death of Major General Nathanael Greene, a Revolutionary war hero awarded Mulberry Grove Plantation for his service during the war. By all accounts, he was one of George Washington's best officers and the husband of Catherine "Caty" Greene. They worked the plantation together until Nathanael died suddenly from sunstroke. In desperation, Caty began working the land by herself, until one day, she met a young man who was tutoring her neighbor's children. The man's name was Eli Whitney.

Whitney moved onto the plantation to work on his inventions, one of which was expected to help Caty process her crop of short staple cotton. Together, they put the finishing touches on one of history's greatest inventions, the cotton gin.

According to the Wikipedia entry for Caty Greene, it is widely believed she actually provided a great deal of input for the device. However, Eli received sole credit as social norms inhibited women from filing patents at the time.

With the development of gin technology, Savannah moved away from a small military settlement into a vibrant city. Developers and fortune seekers, along with the trades that serviced them, flocked to its shores. Since few people had land or money to move their dead, and so many left unclaimed, the city simply built over them.

Many believe this was the final act to set the wheels in motion. Savannah had developed a psychic disassociation and sense of amnesia about its dead.

Eventually, the city recovered from its neurosis and not only acknowledged death, but also paved the way for America to celebrate it as an extension of life during the Victorian era and even into modern times. A grand example of this can be viewed at beautiful *Bonaventure Cemetery*, which ironically translates, *Good Fortune.*

The emerging funeral parlor industry helped drive ease of burial, taking much of the responsibility for dealing with deceased loved ones away from the family and placing it in the hands of professionals. With this newfound free time, it became not only acceptable to memorialize the dead, but to celebrate their life graveside.

This new culture gave sculptors, like John Walz, a stage to display their memorial craft and Bonaventure residents like Savannah poet, Conrad Aiken, socially acceptable latitude to infuse creativity into the monuments representing them. Aiken's tombstone was carved into a bench so that people could rest while they visited, watch the ships leaving the harbor, and enjoy a Martini with their picnic lunch as was Conrad's custom during his life.

Today Savannah's dead *are* remembered; visits to Bonaventure Cemetery thrive, famous lives are retold in books and on tours in the city. Others are recognized for different reasons, those who loved Savannah too much, died tragically, or left behind worldly business so pressing they refuse to move on to the next phase. Their stories are commemorated nightly throughout the city in any number of humorous, somber or chilling tales.

Savannah's polarized attitude toward death, from passive denial to open celebration, seems to have exacerbated the rift in the underworld...bringing it to a constant fluid state. This jagged ethereal motion expanded Savannah's borders beyond just a *port* city; it was now a *portal* city as well.

'the 1790' ✦

K illing one's self over unrequited love has always been extremely fashionable in Savannah. Sitting a half block away from *Colonial Park Cemetery* is a story straight from "Page 6".

The 17Hundred90 is an anomaly (hereafter referred to as 'the 1790'). Originally built in 1820, it avoided using the year as its namesake due to the large number of tragedies that befell the city that year.

Besides the great yellow fever epidemic, the area also suffered a massive fire in January. Savannah was the eighteenth largest city in the United States, until the blaze destroyed much of it. The flames moved quickly, and by the time they had reached Ellis Square, they had ignited a storehouse of gunpowder that set off part of Savannah like a bomb. In modern terms that would equate to half of Detroit, Michigan going up in a single, disastrous burst.

While the 1790 was able to escape the earthly markings of tragedy, it has not been able to escape the spiritual ones. Rather, it seems to have gotten the double portion. The 1790 has the most requested haunted room in the city. Room 204.

Amateur paranormal investigators, thrill seekers, even Miley Cyrus have requested the famed quarters hoping to have their own brush with one of Savannah's most famous ghosts, Anna.

When we interviewed the current owner, Patrick Godley, on our pod-casts, he was quick to admit the details are scarce but the fact remains, a young girl does haunt the inn. He also conceded the reason *why* Anna haunts the 1790 is a mystery.

Some accounts say she was a servant girl, impregnated by a young sailor, who flung herself from room 204 after he abandoned her for another port of call. In another version, Anna was leaving with the young sailor but the owner of the inn prevented it. In this explanation, the owner of the inn was likely her husband and he locked her in the room causing her untimely jump. Or push, as some speculate.

Anna doesn't just have an affinity for room 204; she also seems to have an affinity for women's finery. Jewelry and clothing (particularly undergarments) are often discovered in places other than their original location. Patrick informed us, when Miley and her mother were in Savannah filming *The Last Song*, Miley's mother requested room 204.

Before bed, Miley laid out an outfit for the upcoming shoot, which began early the next morning on Tybee Island. She had a pair of boots with her as well, but they stayed buried deep in her luggage. Apparently, Anna took a liking to the boots. When Miley woke, she found them lying on top of her suitcase with a small wet handprint on one. Miley posted the events on *Twitter* while at the inn, and Patrick was left to field questions and phone calls about the incident for weeks after it happened.

Before Miley left, she signed the journal in room 204. The piano player at the time, who has since passed on, decided the paper was a keepsake and didn't want it stolen. She tore the page out of the journal and took it home with her. Weeks later, she called Patrick very excited and agitated, claiming the piece of paper had mysteriously disappeared. She was convinced Anna had followed her home to reclaim it. Upon investigation, the staff of the 1790 discovered the piece of paper had in fact reappeared. It was located behind the front desk and laminated for safekeeping, a memento of the experience.

The haunted events at the 1790 are not isolated to room 204. The kitchen staff report aggressive activity...more than simply moving objects. One member of the kitchen staff was locked in the walk-in cooler. His attempts to use the safety handle proved futile and the cook was stuck inside for several minutes. He was petrified when he emerged and convinced there was no other explanation than his having angered the previous cook in some way.

Patrick has happened upon his own experiences since taking over the 1790 in October of 2010. He believes it's possible that a young African-

American boy, feasibly a former slave, harmlessly haunts the inn and enjoys returning found money, particularly pennies. When he first took over, he would find pennies in odd places, like in the brick mortar. He reported pennies continued to show up for twenty-eight days in a row, when no one else was around. He theorized the young boy returns the money, because as a slave he could have gotten into serious trouble for keeping it hidden. Even a penny might have been construed as a plan or means to escape.

Regardless of the specifics behind the stories at the 1790, the ghosts seem to have received the Godley family with open arms. The Inn is a favorite among local tour operators due to the large number of paranormal photos produced both inside and when telling the stories in front of it.

If you decide to find out for yourself, book ahead and according to most reports, stay for at least two nights. In every account I've heard personally, a brush with Anna happened on the second night. If a traveling sailor scorned her, it would make sense she would be leery of strangers and perhaps need a little time to get used to their presence before making hers known.

If you do stay, remember to sign the journal and keep a watchful eye on your undergarments. Anna may decide to borrow them.

The 17hundred90 Restaurant and Inn is located at 307 East President Street and can be reached by calling (912)-236-7122 or by visiting 17hundred90.com.

old CANDLER ✦

On the Drayton Street side of Forsyth Park sits 110,000 square feet of *paranormal playground.* The old Candler Hospital is Georgia's oldest hospital. It is located in the southernmost portion of the historic district and its presence there is a matriarchal reminder of Savannah's beginnings. It has seen more tragedy than any other single location within the city and remains one of the best photo opportunities for paranormal anomaly, especially images of what appear to be bodies hanging from the nearly three hundred year old Candler Oak.

The hospital was founded in 1803 as a Seamen's Hospital and poorhouse. In 1808, it became known as the Savannah Poorhouse and Hospital Society. It received its present-day name in 1931, when acquired by the Methodist Church. The name was changed to honor Bishop Warren Candler.

During the Civil War, the hospital was used for both Confederate and Union troops. The Candler Oak was a stockade area for Yankee soldiers. The tree was often used to carry out hangings on the condemned. Inside they were treated poorly as well; in large part because the South was under a blockade and supplies, even for Southerners, were scarce. Many of the sick and wounded Northern troops died from lack of treatment and dysentery.

The hospital is comprised of two buildings that were used as a United States Customs Laboratory and the Tidelands Community Mental Health Center. The Georgia State Board of Pardons and Paroles was the last tenant. Since then, renovation plans have stalled and deals to purchase the hospital have fallen through while the ghostly activity born from tragedy continues.

The most famous part of the hospital for the paranormal enthusiasts is the morgue tunnel, or its proper name, the *dead room*. Before the days of refrigeration, bodies had to be kept in a cool dark place until they could be prepared for burial. This was the original purpose for the tunnel at its busiest period in 1876, during one of the many yellow fever epidemics. During this time, nearly three hundred people died in one 48-hour interval at the hospital. Savannah still reeled from the 1854 epidemic, and moved into full-blown panic at the prospect of another one. Sadly, it was not spared.

In the spring of 1876, the customary deluge poured down on the low country. Record highs were recorded as the temperature soared into the 90's and eighteen inches of rain fell in only sixteen days. The dampness, mold and mosquitos all found the needed prerequisites to thrive. By August of 1876, it became clear Savannah was in for yet another horrific yellow fever epidemic.

Based on the records available, in just four months, one out of every six people that remained in the city died from the disease. Victims complained of symptoms including a burning thirst, bleeding lips and exhibited a light brown fur on their tongues. Most of the victims that did not recover died within three to five days.

Savannah received help from all over the world. Countries as far away as France donated food, medicine and supplies. Available doctors reported visiting over one hundred people per day and the morning news announced people sought relief through drugs and religion. Several people overdosed on *Laudanum* (Opium tincture) and churches opened their doors so people could appeal to God for relief twenty-four hours a day.

It was widely speculated, people rather than insects were the carriers of the disease, causing suspicion and paranoia to grow unrestrained. As much as half of Savannah's 30,000 inhabitants fled the city, almost all of them white. The African-American population, many without means to travel stayed behind, practicing their own preventative measures to guard against the fever. This included adorning their doors and windows with *"Haint Blue"* paint because they believed it resembled the ocean and evil spirits were unable to cross water.

This practice appeared to work as death rates among the colored population were significantly lower than for whites. However, it was decades before they discovered it was not a spiritual effect of the blue paint, but a key ingredient that kept the mosquitos at bay. Turpentine.

While a curfew was imposed on the rest of the city, wagons pulled up to Candler Hospital and the dead cargo was loaded. The wagons made their way down the dark, desolate, bumpy back roads of the low country. The ghoulish drivers sought the loved ones of the deceased and once found, would quickly unload the body for burial. When they were unable to locate family members, they would bring them back to the hospital. Eventually, under pressure to have the burials completed by sunrise, they began burying some of the victims illegally in and around the hospital property. A number of these bodies were found during Savannah's development and we know the burials were unauthorized. There was never a charter for cemeteries that far south in the historic district.

One of the odder things I have noticed when I take guests to the Candler Hospital area are intense but small areas of extreme cold spots. Occasionally a guest will complain of feeling extremely thirsty and appear flushed. It's hard not to recall the primary symptoms of yellow fever and wonder if these folks are experiencing the energy and lingering feelings of those who died at the hospital. Electronic equipment failure is not unheard of at Candler but in my experience, it is rare. However, it remains one of the best spots in the city for those interested in electronic voice phenomenon (EVP). I always encourage guests and visitors to turn on their phone recorder during that portion of the tour. Many have communicated surprise and shock at what they heard on the playback.

After spending so much time in and around the Candler Hospital area, I was bound to have my own experience. It happened on a balmy night in August of 2010. I was talking to a group of about twenty-five people and the humidity in the area was nearly unbearable. I always carry bottled water with me on the tour and between stories; I do my best to stay hydrated in the sweltering heat.

Once we reached the hospital, I laid my bottled water next to me as I disclosed the story and history of old Candler. As I was talking, I felt the right side of my body go completely ice cold for a little more than a second. It was a scary event, as the coldness seemed to pass through me, or at least half of me, it gave the impression of a very human-like shape.

I finished the story and encouraged everyone to explore the space around the hospital, taking photos and recordings if they were so inclined. I reached for the bottle of water that had been on the same side of my body that had gone ice cold. I took a large drink of the water but immediately spewed it out of my mouth and onto the exposed back of a woman wearing a spaghetti strapped top. I attempted to recover, profusely apologized, and was so embarrassed I assured her I would refund her money for the tour. What I didn't tell her or anyone else on the tour was the reason I had spit the water back out. It wasn't because it had gone down the wrong way…whatever had passed through me, had traveled thru the water as well and the effects had left it bitter and foul.

I was immersed in the taste of wormwood and malignant vinegar on my pallet for the remainder of the tour. To make matters worse, my water was spoiled making me certain I would dehydrate; even if I didn't die from whatever the spirit had left behind.

Thankfully, that was the next to the last stop on the tour and I was able to make it until the end. I have to admit, I did not give a very good tour, and I was not very friendly afterword. I wasn't in the slightest mood to stay and talk with guests as I usually am. I kept the bottle and took it home with me. I felt chilled and sick for the rest of the night. I laid the bottle on my desk and finally drifted off to sleep.

I woke up the next morning feeling a little better; only a slight ache in my muscles that is customary with mild dehydration. As I walked to the refrigerator to get a cold bottle of water, then over to my desk to check my e-mail, I couldn't help but notice the bottle of water I had on the tour with me the night before. The water in the bottle had already begun to change. It was turning a grotesque brown with an almost unperceivable green and becoming some slightly thicker mystery liquid.

It was two days before I flushed the water down the toilet. In those two days, I watched the water turn almost completely brown including a slight trace of black. The odor was unlike anything I have ever smelled; there's nothing I can compare to it. If pressed to give a description I suppose I can only speculate…in my darkest imagination, it might be like drinking the pus from a gangrenous wound.

The few people I have told that story, the ones I have trusted with it, always ask me why I didn't have the water tested. My answer is the same every time, it's easy for you to ask because you aren't the one who drank it, and the truth of the matter is, I don't really want to know.

séance MAN ✦

The large, black "*OLAF OTTO*" safe daringly sits unattended on the sidewalk in front of Bradley's Lock and Key paying homage to times gone by. It stands as an overt advertisement for the safety of, well, safes.

The black and white lettering on the cloudy glass storefront offers services (*Safes Opened, Combinations Changed*). There are two marker boards on the white building, one dedicated to the date of the building (1855) and the other to the founding of Bradley's (1883).

The three of us shook out our umbrellas before walking through the front entrance to escape the Saturday afternoon thunderstorm. The owner, William Houdini Bradley greeted us.

He's a soft-spoken man with sharp eyes and a mischievous smile. His 78 years have been kind. His hair is intact and near its original charcoal color. Mr. Bradley is used to visitors and was welcoming, almost expectant, as we entered unannounced with a camera and voice recorder.

The smell of old wood and locksmith oil stimulated my senses in tandem. Three walls were completely covered with countless keys; their layers marking the longevity of Bradley's like the exposed rings of a fallen tree. A massive antique cash register, the first cash register of *The Byrd Cookie Company*, sat atop a table cluttered with loose keys that had escaped the wall.

Mr. Bradley's wife sat at a desk against the keyless back wall. The desktop was buried in handwritten work orders. An old landline telephone on the desk began to ring. "Wow, that is a really old phone," I said to Mr. Bradley's wife as the receptionist sidestepped the back of the chair to answer it.

"It sure is. The phone service is still in Simon Bradley's name, William's grandfather," she replied. "Really? How long has the phone been in his name?" I wondered aloud. "For as long as you have been able to get telephones," she replied confidently. "We just never changed it over."

Mr. Bradley began to guide us through the beautiful mess. The first stop was a stack of orange café counter chairs. He paused to stare at them before telling their story, "I bought these for a dollar a piece when McCrory's closed." He wiped the dust off and gratuitously rearranged the chairs from one disorganized pile into another. He continued,

"W.W. Law came in here one day and told me he knew where I got these chairs," Mr. Bradley said calmly. Satisfied with the new arrangement, he pushed his hair back into a part. "It seems there were six black men who refused to get up from the counter and off of these very chairs. They would come in everyday and ask to be served and sat there waiting. They never got served but after two weeks, they did get arrested."

I had heard this story before. W.W. Law was also known as "Mr. Civil Rights" and was the President of the Savannah Chapter of the NAACP until 1976. These chairs were emblematic of the civil rights movement in Savannah. It seemed fantastic that Mr. Bradley would have the chairs just sitting there gathering dust in a mismatched pile. It would be like having the Rosa Parks bus seats in a Montgomery stockroom. It seemed even odder that W.W. Law had apparently made no effort to acquire them. However, such is Bradley's Lock and Key, treasures are common and everything is history.

Mr. Bradley paused to stare at the chairs and said, "One day I am going to clean them up and donate them to the museum." Things started to make sense with that statement. It satisfied me, and I am guessing it satisfied W.W. Law as well. Mr. Bradley is well liked and respected. I concluded, just as W.W. Law must have, if Mr. Bradley was emphatic one day they would be in the museum, they will.

As we continued the tour, we stopped in front of several family photos. The stories shifted from the treasures of the shop to the treasures of the family, his grandchildren. He began to tell us about their academic accomplishments with the predictable pride of a doting grandfather. As I listened, one of my companions nudged me and nodded toward a side-wall. There is an old sign from the original Bradley's, again offering services: "*Expert – Safe. Gun. Pistol. Umbrella – Repair.*"

"You repaired umbrellas, Mr. Bradley?" I inquired. "Oh yeah, umbrellas used to be big business," he said, amused by my surprise. I tried to contemplate a time when umbrellas were so expensive and of such quality, it made more sense to repair than replace them.

The thought was cut short as we moved toward the back wall and the purpose of our visit. Hanging next to a room rate card for *The Marshall Hotel*, advertising rooms from $2 to $4, is a vintage photo of Mr. Bradley's namesake, Harry Houdini. Houdini stands with his wife, wearing his customary long coat and bowtie, hat in hand. The photographers mark is "NICE 12-6-1". A mere thirteen years before Houdini's death.

Here, in this back corner, we found another reminder of the Houdini-Bradley connection. Harry Houdini was deeply involved in spiritualism, mysticism, and was one of the great debunkers of charlatans. William Bradley's father, Aaron, was deeply involved in spiritualism, hypnotism and séances. He was close to the Houdini family, eventually naming his son William Houdini Bradley, now shortened to "Dini" by those closest to him.

Aaron was apparently adept at his craft and taught his other son, Eddie, to hypnotize himself. This practice is credited with transforming Eddie into an accomplished competitive marksman and champion weightlifter. "Eddie used to stand right there and use a safe against that back wall as a target," the receptionist pointed out with a sly grin. "My God," I remarked, clearly astonished. Everyone in the shop smirked at my surprise; it was altogether mundane to them.

I couldn't help but imagine this building a generation before Aaron inherited it, when target practice was still condoned in the front room. Mr. Bradley also told us stories of Aaron attempting to contact Houdini after his death, on behalf of the family. The séances conducted would have made Houdini himself proud and is probably why Bradley's Lock and Key is haunted.

The front door is well-known for opening and closing on its own. Perhaps a former customer, now departed, coming to sit and pass the time or pick up a set of extra keys for a storage room....

Objects are notoriously credited with holding the energy of their former owners and attracting spirits. The program *Haunted Collector* is built entirely upon this premise and Bradley's has no shortage of antique go-to items for would-be ghosts.

Ryan Dunn of *3D Ghost Hunters* has done quite a few quality investigations in Savannah. During an interview with me on *Savannah Shadows*, he noted the high quality EVP's they had picked up during the Bradley investigation. Others have seen men dressed in nineteenth century attire entering and leaving the building.

In my mind, I couldn't help but entertain the extraordinary. What if the ghostly activity is none other than the great Houdini? Why not? The families have several "key" things in common. The Bradley family is a three-generation safe cracking outfit and Harry Houdini apprenticed as a locksmith, a handy skill in his escape routines. Aaron was an accomplished séance-man. And let's face it, Houdini never shied away from a crowd in this life. It made sense he might follow the same calling in the next one too.

Unavoidably, I began to wonder, did Aaron ever contact Houdini from Bradley's? We know he tried. What developed from the séances at the shop? What if Houdini's wife had attended? Perhaps she would have heard the elusive password, *Rosebud....*

I tried to listen to Mr. Bradley talk about lesser objects around the Houdini photograph but it was futile. Should I suggest Harry himself might be responsible for the haunting? For the moment, I decided against it. The Bradley's hadn't been shy about sharing stories. Surely, they would have already suggested it. On the other hand, maybe, like everything else, they were waiting for me, so they could watch me marvel one last time at the endless possibilities contained here.

"Do you think one of the ghosts here might be Houdini?" I finally asked, hoping to clear the 500-pound gorilla in the conversation. (All around laughter) "Weelllll, I guess anything is possible." It was clear to me I was in the land of *Pure Imagination* and Mr. Wonka wasn't going to surrender his mantle of mystery. In true Houdini fashion, he left me to wonder.

However, belief in a Houdini presence doesn't just rest with me. Extended members of the Houdini family have visited Bradley's as well. Hardeen Harry Houdini, the great-nephew of Harry, dropped by the curious store to learn more about his great uncle and perhaps attempted to discern his presence. It would appear, he is a believer, carrying on the Houdini tradition as a traveling magician and illusionist with his wife.

The Houdini-Bradley connection is unquestioned. The fact that the place is haunted is uncontested. However, is the spirit at the curious store The Great Harry Houdini? It's probably folly to discuss it, but it is endlessly entertaining to speculate.

So are most things at Bradley's Lock and Key.

the EVIL SHADE ❧

Wright Square was one of Savannah's four originals along with Telfair, Ellis and Johnson. It also served as the judicial center. A person could be indicted, held, tried and have their sentence carried out all in one place. Hangings were public events and it was from the end of one of these ropes that Alice Riley would find her way into history.

Alice was one of the first indentured servants James Oglethorpe bought for the sum of approximately eight dollars. When she arrived in the city, she was placed in the bond of a particularly crass and perverse man, William Wise.

Wise was a man of low regard but an artificially inflated self-esteem. He carried himself as a man about town even though his position in the community was known as "the cow keeper".

Alice was placed with him to assist with the livestock and the even more loathsome task of bathing her master. Wise laid back and his long stringy hair would fall into a bucket of water. Alice, still a teenager, was forced to pick the knots out of his hair, wash it, bathe him and attend to his every whim.

Those whims are speculation at best, but as James Caskey points out on page 105 of his book *Haunted Savannah: The Official Guidebook to Savannah Haunted History Tour*, Wise had already tried to bring a prostitute into Savannah posing as his daughter.

Alice Riley is often referred to as *Sorceress* Alice Riley in Savannah, but as Caskey points out, there doesn't seem to be any evidence she practiced witchcraft and it certainly wasn't the crime for which she was hanged. That would be the murder of one William Wise, carried out with the help of a man named Richard White, widely considered the common law husband of Alice.

The plan was a simple one. They waited until Wise called Alice in for his regular bath and grooming session. Once his head was leaned back into the bucket of water, Alice and Richard held him under until he drowned.

The two apparently dumped the body in the Savannah River but failed to consider the current. Instead of drifting down the river, the body is said to have simply floated across it and washed up on the opposite shore. The crime was quickly discovered and both Richard and Alice were convicted of murder. Sentenced to hang, they were kept in the simple one story jail located at the northwest corner of the square.

Hangings were a straightforward affair in those times. The body could be left for three days as a sobering reminder to would be lawbreakers. Alice's hanging would have been routine except for one problem; she was found to be pregnant.

Again, speculation surely enters. Was the father of the child Richard White or William Wise? If it was Wise's child, a likely conclusion could be drawn which brought new light to Alice and Richard's actions.

In either case, Alice was imprisoned until she gave birth to the baby, who was immediately taken from her. She would never hold her child and now, the gallows awaited her arrival. She walked into Wright Square on January 19, 1735 and was hanged by the neck until dead for the crime of murder. Her body dangled there for three days. She had become the first woman executed in Georgia.

Her baby would die less than two months later.

Today the story is remembered, not just in historical and legal records, but also by those who say they have encountered the ghost of Alice. It is a common occurrence for people visiting Wright Square to tell stories of a frantic woman looking for her child.

The woman, in period dress, has even been mistaken for an actor by some who say the apparition approached them in broad daylight and was as solid as a living person. It's only when she disappears into nothingness, while continuing her desperate search around the square, that the witnesses realize they have seen her ghost.

The credibility for the claims I have heard, rests in the fact that many of the people who have contact with the ghost of Alice are not from Savannah. They are visitors, most for the first time, and none I have spoken with heard her story beforehand. However, an overwhelming number of the witnesses did have one commonality; they were women with child in a stroller.

Further evidence of an unjust hanging, many say, is the fact that Spanish moss won't grow on the north side of the square where the gallows were. Conditions for Spanish moss are ideal in Wright Square and it thrives on the southern end. There doesn't appear to be a botanical reason for the limitation. Is there a spiritual boundary line in the square; the north end cut off from normal acts of nature by the ethereal residue of zealous lynch mobs?

Spanish moss is neither Spanish, nor moss. It is actually a member of the same family as the pineapple and draws its nutrients from the air and moisture around it. It is prevalent throughout Savannah and used for a variety of things in the low country. It is considered a sacred staple item in potions, magic oils and is used as a traditional stuffing in Voodoo dolls.

Could this sacred plant, which takes nothing from the tree on which it abides, be unwilling to grace those unjust voids where innocent blood was shed?

Its absence in the gallows section of Wright Square seems to say it will not.

sorrel-WEED ❧

Your first experience with the Sorrel-Weed House probably came during the opening scene of *Forrest Gump*, where the feather is floating effortlessly against a cloudless sky. That movie moment was shot from the roof of this home. It was very peaceful, wasn't it? Well, don't get used to it because the serenity ends there.

This Greek revival masterpiece created a perfect storm for one of the most haunted residences in the country. It's a story of probable murder, certain suicide and Revolutionary War era bodies found during a 1996 renovation.

It continues to rear its massive paranormal head nightly to hopeful guests that pay to walk through its haunted hallways. EMF detectors are provided by the staff and it is often a cramped affair.

The Sorrel-Weed House was completed in 1840(ish) by famed architect, Charles Cluskey. The home is perhaps the only home in existence that played host to Union General, William Tecumseh Sherman and Confederate icon, Robert E. Lee. It saw some of the grandest social gatherings in nineteenth century Savannah. Today, it survives as one of the most famous historical markers in Georgia's first city. However, it's the haunted history of Sorrel-Weed that continues to bring the curious.

The house has been investigated by multiple paranormal-reality programs and conducts haunted tours through its grandiose rooms on a nightly basis. Bradley Dilling, the night manager and head 'ghost host' at Sorrel-Weed, appeared on our radio program to offer some insight into the events and relate a few personal stories from guests.

Bradley told us the paranormal activity can be traced to Francis Sorrel who was a shipping magnate and one of the wealthiest men in Savannah. Francis reportedly started an affair with a Haitian slave girl named Molly. She was in her early twenties and quite beautiful. Likely, she reminded Francis of his childhood in Haiti where he was born to a wealthy plantation owner.

Eventually Matilda, his wife, discovered the affair. According to some reports, she was mentally unstable even before the betrayal. Unable to reconcile, she plunged to her death from the main house. The jump snapped her neck. Very shortly afterward, Molly was found with her neck broken as well. She was hanged in the carriage house.

Controversy continues to surround these events. I conducted a cursory web search after interviewing Bradley and revealed many strong opinions.

Even if we take the main story about the Sorrel-Weed House at face value, it doesn't explain the mystery...did Matilda commit suicide, if so, was it because she found out about the infidelity? Was Molly murdered? Could Francis have committed the heinous crime? If so, what was his motivation? Was he attempting to avoid the shame of having an interracial affair that caused his wife's suicide? Even from a historical perspective, there are many unanswered questions. The paranormal discussion takes us deeper still.

The most famous paranormal event documented at the Sorrel-Weed, made such an impact it has become a part of the customary tour. It is an EVP of what appears to be a woman with a Haitian accent pleading for help, begging for her life. The T.A.P.S. crew captured the recording while filming a Halloween special.

Many people believe the recording is a sound bite from Molly's murder, forever repeating itself in a tragic ethereal loop. Often people who take the tour excuse themselves during this portion, saying the screams are too disturbing to hear.

The main case for murder rests in the fact, the most common types of suicide in Haiti deal with the shedding of blood, such as slitting the wrists. It isn't likely a slave would choose a Colonial noose; a symbol of terror and degradation by white owners, as a proper method for ending their own life.

Camera and equipment failures are so common, Bradley asks everyone to check their battery strength before the tour so they don't have to second guess whether it was charged or not.

Grabbing is another common phenomena reported. A Baptist minister and his son reported feeling a body-shaped form sit down between them on a couch in the home. The pair were so shaken by the event the man remarked to Bradley, "I am a minister and do not believe in things of this nature, but this house has given me something to think about." Sorrel-Weed has given many something to think about, including a few folks who accompanied me on a private walk-thru one evening after the home closed for the night.

It was a balmy August evening and Bradley had invited us to do a follow up interview to the radio show. I brought my videographer and the show's co-host. We didn't know how much access Bradley would grant us, but we came prepared. We brought a few staple investigation items including a Flir i7 thermal imager, which is the Mercedes of thermal imaging for paranormal investigations. It is also the brand used by the United States military.

Bradley welcomed us as we climbed the front steps to enter the blessed coolness of the foyer. He looked disheveled after doing three tours to capacity crowds. He started his fourth tour until we put him at ease, explaining he could take us straight to the money shots. That would be the room where Matilda jumped and the carriage house where Molly was found hanged. Bradley seemed relieved.

First up, the carriage house, site of the famed EVP. I immediately pulled out the Flir and started taking readings. Nothing unusual. I switch to the Tri-Field EMF meter.

*** For readers who do not participate in paranormal investigations, I feel it would be useful to briefly explain what the EMF meter is used for.

A Tri-Field meter will measure three different waves: magnetic, radio/microwave and electronic. The one I use (100XE) is a 3-axis meter, which means it "looks" up and down, left and right, backward and forward. That is useful because it doesn't matter how you hold the meter.

How is it used in paranormal work?

The Magnetic setting is the most useful. A good meter will read 0–100 milligauss. Most household appliances like AC wall adaptors, TV's, radios, or household appliances will register 10 or more milligauss.

You can make sure your meter is working by testing it on objects that would surely register 10 or above like the ones listed above. Once you know the EMF device is reading properly switch to the low readings setting (0-3).

Entities are believed to emit energy, a field, or an aura. Human being's conduct a very low reading but only certain instruments can detect it... like sharks. They can detect magnetic fields when the great conductor, salt water, further enhances them. When a spirit is unencumbered by a body, its energy field is believed to be higher than ours but lower than appliances and can be picked up by looking in the 0-3 milligauss range.

*Keeping the sensitivity in this range shields you from false positives that would read 10 or higher because you have excluded them via the 0-3 setting. Instead, it would now indicate an uncommon or anomalous magnetic field coming from somewhere...or some**thing**.*

This kind of thinking developed when early after-life researchers tried incorporating scientific methods into their experiments and noticed that EVPs and ghostly photos were almost always connected with a preceding EMF reading in that peculiar 0-3 milligauss zone.

All that said, I turned on the EMF meter. Nothing.

The oppressive humidity shortened my patience. "How about we head to Matilda's room?" I asked and Bradley agreed.

We made our way back to the main house and upstairs to Matilda's quarters on the second floor. The eerie light of the full moon saturated the room. I hadn't noticed it was full until I saw its bluish glow against the antique aura of the walls.

Bradley slipped into 'auto-guide' mode as I continued to move around the room with the mute, useless EMF detector. I silently cussed it and wiped the sweat from my forehead. I could hear Bradley behind me answering the same questions he gets every night, *ad infinitum*.

He told us he felt a sort of kindred spirit with the supernatural residents of the property. Bradley is a sincere person. One of the good guys in the Savannah paranormal scene. I thought he might be up for some theorizing, so I asked if he would be willing to call upon them for us.

Nothing else was panning out and we were on a limited timeframe.

"Sure, I'll give it a try," Bradley answered as he walked, almost instinctively, to the place where Molly was hanged. He seemed a little shy speaking to the spirits in front of a crowd but it was obvious to me he was telling the truth; he had done this before.

I walked over to Bradley slowly, EMF meter in hand. I wanted to be respectful of the situation but I also needed to take measurements. Still nothing. When Bradley came to a natural pause, I suggested I lay the EMF meter on the windowsill, which would allow me to step away from Bradley and the process. Bradley said a few things, asked if they were pleased with how he was telling their stories, asked if they had anything they wanted to say or if they could show a sign they were listening. Nothing. Finally, Mark suggested Jenny, my co-host, try it.

Jenny Wright came to Blue Orb and Savannah through a strange series of events and she had quickly developed a reputation as a gifted intuitive. This wasn't a formal investigation so I was prepared to tread on ground I usually shied away from, the psychic approach.

I haven't had much luck employing psychics in investigations. I'm not insinuating it doesn't work, but you have to be extremely careful who you ask to participate, especially in Savannah. Here we have everything from *the real* to the Stockholm certifiable kook. I was comfortable with Jenny and wanted to take advantage of the private access so graciously provided. I looked at Jenny and she indicated she would try.

She approached the window area slowly, prayerfully with her fingers interlocked and held in front of her waist. Standing next to the window, she stared outside and began asking the usual questions I hear from most psychics, "Is there anything you would like to say...Is anyone here?"

The thermal began showing a significant drop in temperature. 83 degrees, which is significant in a room reading in the 90's just moments before. I aimed the thermal at the window and watched as a slender, but undeniably human, form appeared against the glass. 78 degrees. It was not visible to the naked eye but it was unmistakable through the eyes of the Flir. I didn't say a word. I had seen too many investigations blown by the inevitable *Holy shit, look at this* comment.

I took image after image. Mark knew something was happening and looked at me pointedly. He's been on many of those blown investigations so true to form; he held his tongue and allowed the situation to unfold. Experienced investigators make all the difference in those situations.

Jenny was completely unaware of what I was capturing but she knew something was there as well. She whispered, "Someone is here." I continued taking stills and captured the form as it dissipated. It left much quicker than it had come. Once it was completely gone, I said, "Hey, check this out."

We scrolled through the glowing thermal images several times watching the purple and pink glowing form. It slowly reshaped from mist to full form and then back to mist again, until it disappeared. There was dead silence. The room was as dead and still as the EMF meter still lying on the windowsill.

"I guess that was Molly," Mark said. "Yeah, and I guess sometimes it helps to have a psychic," I responded quietly.

The thermal images may be viewed at savannahshadows.com under the Story Photos tab.

savannah's AMITYVILLE ✦

In September of 2011, we interviewed Christopher Lutz on a podcast episode of *Savannah Shadows*. Lutz is a child survivor of the home featured in *The Amityville Horror*. The Lutz family lasted twenty-eight days before they were driven out of the home amidst tales of bleeding walls and exorcism. Many believed the house was ripe for a haunting of this magnitude because of the horrific crime committed there on November 13, 1974.

Six members of the DeFeo family were shot while they slept by the sole surviving family member Ronald (aka *Butch*) DeFeo. Ronald was convicted and claimed the devil told him to do it. With Ronald in prison, 112 Ocean Avenue was put up for sale and eventually purchased by Christopher's stepfather, George.

There are major differences between The Amityville movie and the book. Christopher has waged his own campaign to have the real story told, saying the movie is almost unrecognizable to him. He believes the house was indeed haunted; not by a portal to hell, but by the psychic doors opened by George and his occult practices.

During the interview, I couldn't help but draw similarities between Amityville's 112 Ocean Avenue and Savannah's 507 East St. Julian Street. I'm speaking of the Hampton Lillibridge House, which holds the title of, "the most psychically active house in North America" by researchers affiliated with the Rhine Research Center and Duke University.

The three-story New England style house stands out among one of Savannah's older neighborhoods. Like Amityville, it is surrounded by controversial claims and brags many a tale of the supernatural. The most famous advocate of the Hampton haunting was Jim Williams.

Jim earned his fame while living at the Mercer-Williams House. However, before *Midnight in the Garden of Good and Evil* and the murder trials he endured, Jim owned the Hampton Lillibridge House. It was here his reputation as both a restorer of homes and an occultist emerged.

Jim was said to have made several calls to the authorities while living there, claiming an intruder was inside the home. No intruder was ever located. The crew that moved the home to its current location complained of shadow like beings attempting to push them off the roof and pull them down holes in the floor. At least one worker was killed during the renovations.

Yet another kinship with Amityville is both homes have been exorcised. Some close to Jim recall he was concerned the house was going to either drive him crazy or kill him. At his wits end perhaps, Jim sought the help of the local clergy. Episcopal Bishop, Reverend Albert Rhett Stewart, entered the home on December 7, 1963 and performed a forty-five minute *Clearance Ceremony*. The rites are similar to an exorcism but reserved for property; the former is performed on a body vexed by an evil spirit. The particulars are inconsequential, however, because it didn't work. Less than a month later the shadows returned, harassing resident and visitor alike.

Finally, in 1969, Jim moved out of Hampton Lillibridge and into the Williams House. Some people in Savannah speculate the move didn't help because the shadow activity wasn't caused by the house itself, but rather his occult collection.

The extent of that collection is anyone's guess and the particulars are an even deeper mystery. However, his secret meetings with low country conjurer, Lady Minerva, in dark and hidden cemeteries are well documented.

We also know that after Jim's death, Sotheby's sold at auction, a dagger that was reportedly plunged into the Russian mystic Rasputin over two hundred times. The expected price was around $12,000. It sold for $19,000.

Jim was also a Mason, which would make it fair to say he was predisposed to secrecy. Knowing Jim jokingly used the dagger as a letter opener, it isn't hard to imagine as he traveled the world recovering price-

less antiques, he also put his hands in earth, *Indiana Jones: Raiders of the Lost Ark* fashion and retrieved choice occult artifacts as well.

In either case, the activity can't be completely attributed to the occult items. Reports of supernatural activity continued at Hampton Lillibridge, even after the offending articles were removed. On the other hand, I recently spoke with a well-known businessman in Savannah and he told me the current owners do not believe the house is even haunted.

I found it interesting he would say that. The house is apparently up for sale...again...and at a considerable discount.

So far, there are no takers.

A quick Zillow search shows that the home went up for sale in 2008 for 2.9 million dollars. At the time of printing, it was offered at slightly over 1 million dollars.

the PIGEON HUNTER ✤

Most people are surprised to learn that the Mercer-Williams home has a ghost story. It also holds the distinction of being one of the few homes where anomalous photos are captured on the exterior of the home, specifically on the roof.

The dwelling gained prominence in modern times from the best-selling book, *Midnight in the Garden of Good and Evil*, which details the murder trials of Jim Williams. Jim was put on trial for shooting to death a young boy named Danny Hansford, rumored to be his lover.

In 1981, Jim claimed self-defense. The District Attorney refused to buy it and put Jim on trial for murder. Over the course of nearly a decade, Jim endured four agonizing trials.

Georgia had never tried anyone for anything four times. Finally, after one overturned guilty verdict, two mistrials, and a *not guilty*, Jim walked away a free man. Six months after his acquittal, Jim was found dead inside the Mercer-Williams home. Those who had supported Danny at the trial decided Jim had come full circle with justice. He perished in the spot he should have originally...if Danny had only been quicker on the draw.

John Berendt, the author of *Midnight in the Garden of Good and Evil,* was actually in Savannah following another story when the trial started. He observed Jim's story, unaware it would turn into a four-part drama. He naturally realized the eccentric antique dealer and occultist was worth following.

Jim's peculiar behavior and grandiose holiday social gatherings made for a great story. The book sat on the New York Times bestseller list for almost four years before it was made into a major motion picture, directed by Clint Eastwood.

The strange history at the house is not just limited to Jim Williams. As you explore blogs and message boards that mention the Mercer-Williams house, every so often you'll find someone asking about the ghost of a little boy reported there. Occasionally, the post will have an accompanying photo of what appears to be a blonde haired child on the roof.

The story began when a young boy went seventy feet, to the top of the house, with a slingshot in his back pocket. The mission, wait for pigeons to land on the roof then pick them off with small pebbles. This was a common game for little boys in the 1960's. On this strange day, the young boy plunged over the side of the home. He fell directly onto the wrought-iron fence, breaking the tip off one of the spikes.

Some reports say he was found seven feet below in the dry moat area and fell when he lost his balance lunging at a pigeon. The headline for the newspaper article detailing his death stated, *Tragedy Ends Pigeon Hunt*, but many say the story cannot be correct. If he were jumping for a bird, he would have cleared the wrought iron fence.

Today, the home is owned by Jim Williams's sister and is a major tourist attraction in Savannah. Guided tours are conducted through the home on a regular basis. The tour discusses the history and the architecture of John Norris, the man who designed the house. Some of Jim Williams antiques are exhibited for curious tourists as well.

Outside the home, the silent, broken spike isn't discussed, but it stands as the sole reminder of the boy who fell. Those photographing the home from Monterrey Square still capture images of what appears to be a blonde-haired child standing on the roof...perhaps searching for the pigeon that got away.

A sampling of guest photos I am referring to, as well as, the news article can be seen at Savannahshadows.com under the story pictures tab.

the OLD CEMETARY ❧

In 1750, Christ Church established Colonial Cemetery, Savannah's first formal place of burial. The cemetery was the final resting place for members of every vocation and interred victims of every tragedy to befall Georgia's first city.

Today, it is an anchor stop for ghost tours with good reason; Colonial is ground zero in America's most haunted city. When you step through its gates you have officially hedged your paranormal bet, giving yourself the best chance you may ever have to witness an otherworldly occurrence.

A casual walk along the concrete paths transports you past Revolutionary War heroes, victims of yellow fever, suicides, murders and duels. The serene landscape makes it is easy to immerse yourself in the role of respectful observer. The concise walkways are a gratuitous measure however, offering nothing more than a token gesture to stay off the graves. The six-acre park holds approximately 557 grave markers, a pittance to the true body count within Colonial's gates. According to the cemetery's website, archaeologists have confirmed the existence of 8,678 additional graves within the six acres. Attempting to avoid treading on the dead is a futile effort.

Colonial has provided one of the best pieces of video footage ever captured depicting a ghostly encounter. On the final day of 2008, a fifteen year old boy named Jesse Greathouse, ventured into Colonial Park Cemetery armed with nothing more than curiosity and an off the shelf camcorder.

While panning the cemetery, a small child eerily entered the frame, wearing what appeared to be a Victorian sleeping gown. The child ran past several people walking through the cemetery who did not acknowledge him, then suddenly leapt into the bottom branches of a tree. He hung out of sight for several seconds, then dropped to the ground and disappeared. It's thoroughly unnerving.

Those in the paranormal and special effects industry have examined the video as well. Robert Kurtzman's company, *Creature Corps*, sent a group of experts who spent about two hours reviewing the video. *Creature Corps* is responsible for special effects in such movies as *Misery*, *Hostel*, and *Evil Dead*. The "great" paranormal debunker, The Amazing Randy, declares a long-standing offer of one million dollars to anyone who can prove a paranormal event. (He is apparently the judge as well.) He has viewed the video aired by Channel 8 in Cleveland, Ohio. And while no one has been willing to put their professional credibility on the line (or cough up one million dollars) by saying, "Why yes, that is a ghost", they have in my opinion, done something just as telling…they have found no evidence of *fakery*. A Google search using "Jesse Greathouse ghost video channel 8" as your criteria will likely provide the best example of this video. The family does have a copyright on it, so be sure to respect all applicable laws.

Another child phenomenon occurring at the cemetery is simply referred to as the *red girl*. A young girl, transparently red, is captured in photographs, often kneeling in prayer next to headstones or occasionally standing in front of one. There doesn't appear to be any rhyme or reason to which graves she visits and no one seems to have a theory as to who she may have been in life. The fact that she materializes as a child and is appealing to the heavens, has caused some people to speculate the figure may be angelic in nature.

Blue Orb has two tours nightly that visit the gates of Colonial Park Cemetery and the red girl has proven difficult to capture. However, it turned out to be very moving when it happened.

The first incidence occurred as the 9 p.m. City of the Dead tour was finishing a photo opportunity and proceeding to the next location. A young boy in the group appeared curious and asked, "Mom, I didn't think people could be in the cemetery after dark?" His mother looked down at him and said, "They can't sweetie, why?" The boy was undaunted, "Then why is that girl out there?" Finally, his mother and several others in the crowd looked in the direction he had been pointing and a few began taking photographs. Two guests picked up images of a red form with female, childlike features kneeling next to a small black headstone on the western side of the cemetery. The young boy became concerned when the tour began moving to the next location and told his mom the girl was asking him to stay. The guide said it was an emotional moment and some were moved to tears. The mother, in subsequent communications, stated events of this nature were common for her son. To his credit, the guide reported the young boy seemed completely at ease communicating with the spirit.

This particular photo is on our Facebook page as a 'guest submitted' post.

The cemetery has also been the site of some not so friendly occurrences. In his book *Haunted Savannah*, James Caskey details an incident involving a dog found in the cemetery with its throat slashed in 1999. Just a few months later, in April of 2000, a local historian named Elizabeth Piechocinski was walking her dog, Cedric, next to Colonial Park and happened upon a dead goat on a burial slab. The goat's mouth and feet were bound, its throat slashed, and its heart cut out of its chest. Caskey points out, speculations have ranged from Voodoo ceremony, to cruel unthinkable joke, to perhaps even a satanic ritual. I would be willing to rule out any sort of Voodoo. When an animal is sacrificed in authentic Voodoo ritual, no part of the animal goes to waste. In fact, the adherents consume the meat from the animal and the bones are kept for later use. A satanic ritual seems to be the most likely culprit. If the participants who carried out this ghastly act are actual Satanists is anyone's guess, but the ceremony does mimic accounts of similar blood rituals carried out by people who indeed are.

One of the most recent events occurred May 16, 2011 in Tipton St. John, a village in the English County of Devon. Four goats were sacrificed in a similar fashion. Devon lies in an area known for bona fide practitioners of Satanism and in the minds of the residents, there was no question it was a legitimate offering to the dark prince.

Those who work in the cemetery have occasionally, but cautiously, offered their own experiences. The city of Savannah does not allow ghost stories to be told inside Colonial cemetery by tour companies, believing it sensationalizes death. I can agree with that point, but in all fairness, standing over a grave and declaring a spirit disembodied and glory bound, is a fairly sensational claim as well. The main difference being, the latter is a culturally sanctioned 'happy-thought' and stamped with the family's approval. Therefore, when a city employee offers a story about a paranormal experience, it's in hushed tones with disclaimers such as, if you say I said it, I'll call you a liar.

A local photographer had such an encounter recently. The cemetery was closing and an employee instructed the photographer he would have to leave. The two of them began talking and quickly the conversation turned to ghosts. At first, the employee was emphatic he had never had a paranormal experience in the cemetery. Pressed by the photographer, he admitted on several occasions unseen hands had grabbed him and there were certain parts he shied away from, fearing another brush with an invisible force. As unsatisfying as it may be for the reader, I must refrain from revealing the photographers name and especially the city employee, for obvious reasons.

One of the main reasons paranormal enthusiasts like photographing the cemetery is the chance to pick up something beyond the garden-variety orb. One of these things, I simply call the *black shadow* phenomena. It is a large, hulking, dense shadow and many speculate it is the ghost of Rene Rondolia, also known as Savannah's Frankenstein.

While the popular stories about Rene, and even his existence, have been dismantled as hokum by credible historians, the black shadow phenomena continues. It usually shows up lurking amongst the family vaults or in the rear of the cemetery near the Orphan's Wall. The form doesn't appear to be cast at any sort of angle as a normal shadow should. It appears erect and darker than the shadows around it, and it has a human-like shape. The most interesting explanation came courtesy of a man who captured the image on his camera in September 2011. The image showed the customary tall blackness I have become familiar with, but this man's image was uncharacteristically clear and revealed what appeared to be something in the 'hands'. It derailed me for a moment and I stopped mingling with the crowd in order to have a closer look. What the man said affected me. He said, "It is Death." I smiled at him and said, "You mean like the Grim Reaper?" The man looked at me dead-pan and in a heavy Italian accent answered, "Exactly."

In my line of work I have to keep an extremely open mind and remain above all else, nonjudgmental. This man, however, wasn't my usual guest showing me a photo saying, "Wow, this is weird, check it out." He meant to clear up the mystery for me. "What makes you think that?" I asked cautiously. "Well, didn't you say this cemetery had thousands of bodies and many of them died from yellow fever?" he asked rhetorically. "Well, yellow fever came to you, to Savannah, as many epidemics. Death lingers in places like this," he explained in a convincing tone. It made my wheels turn.

The most popular form of death personified is the Grim Reaper, and European imagery depicting the dark-clad, scythe-bearing entity became popular around the time of the Black Death. I had just never made the connection. The newfound thought was cathartic and it thoroughly entertained and creeped me out at the same time. "That is a bold claim," I said decidedly. Normally, I don't go after someone's explanation in that manner, but this guy seemed up to the task and had an original theory I wanted to hear more about. He seemed to take it in stride and said, "Tobias, I am very interested in the paranormal. I have done quite a bit of research on this and there are many accounts in villages and towns all over Italy about this sort of thing. These locations are all in areas that suffered heavily during the time of the plague and I have captured many images very similar to this one. What I have here in this image, is Death." After a thinking pause, I inquired sarcastically, "Well, in most theories, God is the only thing omnipresent; how can Death reap the newly departed, show up in Italy and still make it in time for my tour?" "You are joking with me and that is fine, but you are looking at this the wrong way. It is not Death as one person or entity, it is the essence of Death manifest by its many appearances here. This cemetery has many spirits who haven't 'crossed-over', just like the plague lands of Europe. So when you see this thing, when you see Death lingering, it is not concerned with you or me. It is here to attend to business," he said with finality.

Wow. Maybe this iconic cemetery *is* one of Death's favorite haunts. It is fascinating to consider as we close the gates of Colonial Park Cemetery.

the WEEPING SQUARE ✈

A few miles outside of Savannah sits the former site of the Ten Broeck Racetrack. It was the location of the largest slave sale in Georgia history. Known as "The Weeping Time", 436 slaves were sold in a matter of days. Horrific advertisements in the *Savannah Daily Morning News* advertised the upcoming sale of "cotton and Negroes". Potential buyers came from as far away as Virginia, Louisiana and Alabama. The terms of the sale were simple, for four days leading up to the auction, potential buyers had the opportunity to look over slaves held in the horse stables. After that time, the slaves were led to the auction block for bidding.

Unbelievably, Georgia slave auctions were considered more structured and humane than most of their counterparts. A child seven or younger had to be sold with at least one family member. "Lucky" couples who had been together for many years, if married in a Christian church or ceremony by their owner, had to be sold together. If the marriage wasn't recognized by the Christian church, however, the family could be torn apart and sold piece-part to the highest bidder. Under slavery, this is what passed for humaneness and mercy.

Without a doubt, the most famous story to come from this reprehensible sale of human life is the love story of Jeffrey and Dorcas. For Jeffrey, chattel No. 319, marked as a "prime cotton hand," aged 23 years, the competition was high. The first bid was $1,100, and he finally sold for $1,310.

As he readied himself to go with his new owner, he made a humble but unapologetic plea the man also buy Dorcas, the love of his life. Jeffrey quietly submitted no man had ever loved another woman as much as he did Dorcas, and if the new master were willing to buy her also; the two of them, along with their future children would make him fine servants for many years to come.

Jeffrey's new owner agreed to look at Dorcas. They found her standing meekly but resolutely, in front of the man considering her purchase. Jeffrey watched with great anticipation. His new owner finally agreed, providing the bid price was not too high, he would keep them together. However, the sale of Dorcas wasn't until the following day and there was nothing but unimaginable dread to keep either of them company throughout the night.

The next day the sale resumed and ultimately Dorcas made her way to the auction block. The bidding began and Jeffrey was hopeful he would be united with his love. However, it was discovered Dorcas would not be sold alone, but offered as part of a family of four. His new master had no need for the rest of the family and declined to submit the winning bid. Jeffrey and Dorcas would be separated. He would spend his days on the rice plantations of the Great Swamp, while she languished in the cotton fields of South Carolina. The auction block would be the last time they saw one another.

A huge influx of slaves arrived at the same time as Jeffery and Dorcas, in anticipation of the human auction. The usual accommodations, the horse stables, were soon overflowing. Temporary slave pens were used in both Johnson and Calhoun Squares. It is doubtful, those slaves imprisoned in Calhoun Square had any idea they were atop the largest slave cemetery in the country.

Calhoun Square would now have the unique designation of hosting the tragedies of slavery both above and below its grounds. The buildings and homes are all but unchanged since the 1850's and 1860's when they were built. Minus the dumpsters, trash cans and modern vehicles, this square is one of the few places in Savannah you can literally take a 360° view back into time. It is also a place of great mystery and strange occurrences.

It has been remarked, a person with a shovel could very easily find bones in Calhoun Square. A utility company very quickly found this to be true. While installing a new meter, they pulled a skull out of the ground and continued to look on in horror as the other body parts were uncovered. The utility company, after several failed attempts, finally moved the effort. The secret cemetery below the feet of those who relax on the benches, walk dogs or sit on the grass, was once again, left in silence.

Calhoun Square is perhaps the most mysterious square in Savannah, but also one of the least developed. There are no massive monuments and few people know its full history. Despite the lack of recognition, there are more EVP's captured within its borders than any other place in the city.

I have a small hard drive nearly full of ghostly images and eerie recordings submitted by guests of Blue Orb Tours, an overwhelming number from Calhoun Square. Multiple times a week, people send links to audio of strange conversations in broken dialects, weeping and what sounds like the murmuring of crowds. For those unfamiliar with the history, I suggest they may be listening to families as they were torn apart, newly arrived slaves speaking broken English or a West African language…the EVP's begin to make perfect sense.

There is also a *green mist* phenomenon, which floats just above the ground in the square. It resembles a pregnant neon green cloud, arched and hovering around different parts of the area. We have several very good examples of this on our social networking sites.

One photo in particular includes the green mist, along with what appear to be twin girls who have a green tint to their skin, wearing red dresses. The photo shows details down to the ornate buttons. The children appear to be twirling or dancing around a trash can in the square. We have allowed several credible sources to check the photo for manipulation and found none. It's one of the most popular photos in the Blue Orb collection and can be viewed online.

For any would-be paranormal investigators, I recommend visiting with a voice recorder and patience. Recordings present some of the best evidence of paranormal activity and are obviously more credible when you are the one who captures it. Prior to starting Blue Orb, I regarded it as my secret fishing spot. If you are looking to collect your own evidence, sit on a bench for the chance to be amazed.

The standard rules apply: go when the square is quiet and be aware of any unusual noises so you won't confuse them with a possible anomaly.

Calhoun is as close to a sure thing as I know of, and it's absolutely free. All you risk is a little time in a beautiful green space in one of the most picturesque and historical cities in the world.

432 ABERCORN ➤

Sitting silent and alone on the western side of Calhoun Square is perhaps the most controversial home in all of Savannah. A simple Google search reveals the fierce debate that rages around 432 Abercorn. Some say none of the stories are true, others admit their realities were changed by venturing too near. Details are scarce and accurate records hard to come by; this is especially true for the Abercorn House. Tales of supernatural encounters with the home have been passed around for as long as anyone I spoke with could remember. The stories pre-date the advent of the ghost tour industry in Savannah, but sadly, ghost tours have helped contribute to the murky folklore by disseminating massive amounts of false information. In one account, three young girls were murdered inside the home and the bodies posed ritualistically in the form of a triangle. I can safely state…that did not happen.

Some residents, and those with a vested real estate interest, vehemently deny any possibility of paranormal activity and have gone to great lengths to discourage curiosity seekers from taking interest in the property. I can't say I blame them; it could become burdensome living so close to a home with such a storied reputation. For as much as the house is the subject of fanciful tales, however, to suggest that there is absolutely nothing going on at 432 is equally unrealistic. Some residents have been willing to come forward.

A young girl walked up to my tour group in June of 2011 and interrupted me mid-sentence. The twenty-something explained she lived just around the corner and wondered if she might pay to listen to the story.

She had been living in the area for three and a half years. During that time, she had seen crowds from tour companies, countless cars stopping in front of the house, and pedestrians who instinctively paused in front of the home to take snapshots day and night. I declined her offer to pay but invited her to stay and listen. When I finished, I couldn't help but ask if she had an experience with the home she was willing to share. She had not, but her interest peaked when her boyfriend had.

He was in the habit of parking on the street next to the home. When he was approaching, he always sent a text so she could walk downstairs and let him in the security door. He had gone through four cell phones in a little over a year. Each one became hot in his hands as he passed the house while sending the text. Every time, the phone shut down and had to be replaced. When he became aware the house had a long history of strange energy, he began to wonder if that was the reason his phones had failed. As a cautionary measure, he now parks on the other side of the square and texts before he arrives. He's had no further issues with his phone.

Her story didn't surprise me; a great deal of the phenomenon reported is related to electrical equipment failure. We have stopped counting the reports of cameras that have mysteriously shut off or refused to work when attempting to take a photo of the home. Occasionally, the camera felt like it was on fire or "electric" before shutting down. I've received numerous emails from people who have experienced this, stating the camera never worked again after that night.

Physical reactions are also common for those who travel on the sidewalk past the home and even those standing across the street in the square. A quick glimpse of our Facebook page reveals some of those experiences, straight from those who witnessed them.

One of the strangest encounters on my tour happened when a physician reported feeling uncharacteristically ill while simply staring at the house from the square. I noticed he had stepped away from the group and had gone to sit down on a bench while we were talking about the home. Only later would I find out why. The doctor said he began seeing a green hue in front of his eyes and was convinced he was going to lose consciousness. He instinctively moved away from the house for several minutes before regaining his composure. He declined to rejoin the crowd until after we left 432.

His wife actually made the post on Facebook; he was only willing to confirm it happened. She explained he did not have any known pre-existing conditions and he does not drink alcohol. His story in my opinion is among the most credible, of countless tales involving almost identical events, by those you or I might be far less inclined to believe.

Images of a girl about seven years of age are one of the most intriguing phenomena at 432. Generally, the girl appears green and skeletal. Most of these photos show the anomaly in the bottom right window and seem to reveal a face. Closer examination in the daylight reveals a mantelpiece, perhaps of a lion's head, which seems to be the culprit. However, even with that knowledge in hand, the mantelpiece seems to change its facial expression, the direction it is looking and its position on the mantle. This appears to happen even when the photo is taken from the same angle in quick successive exposures.

The idea of a haunted fireplace mantle might seem absurd at first blush but keep in mind there is a popular paranormal theory stating supernatural energy is able to manifest itself through non-organic objects. The popular television show *Haunted Collector* is built upon this premise. Whether the supernatural spirit simply resides within an object or manipulates its shape, it is a widely accepted theory that otherworldly energy is able to dwell in the inanimate. Even the Christian faith teaches the sacrament becomes flesh, the wine becomes blood, and in the cross, there is power. There are stories of God himself indwelling objects, whether temples, arks, or staffs. The Christian faith also teaches negative energy can indwell matter, whether a cloak, a crystal, or a herd of swine.

I put forth the concept not to offend my Christian friends or to reduce their beliefs, but instead to level the playing field. We cannot have it both ways. Either supernatural energy is able to inhabit an object or not. All signs seem to say, yes they can.

Curtains now hang in the peculiar bottom windows as a deterrent to the droves of tourists attempting to capture their own keepsake evidence. Perhaps this would decrease interest in the home if photos of the mantle were the only thing reported, but 432 Abercorn is not a one trick pony.

Another curious event, which occurred during one of our tours, involved witnessing the extremely rare *orb catcher*. Orbs are a commonplace concept in paranormal thought. They are believed to be spirit energy in varying states...in transit, about to manifest, or having recently manifested. The idea of an orb catcher states, supernatural activity in and around a location can become so out of balance with the natural order, the universe will attempt to restore balance by stepping in to assist the paranormal energies (orbs) 'cross-over'. I was familiar with the theories on this phenomenon, but I had never witnessed one firsthand.

I, and about a dozen others, witnessed the orb catcher one night when a man from California captured it in a very odd photo. The crowd actually saw bursts of light coming from behind me several times leading up to the photo being taken; he was the lucky one snapping random shots in hopes of securing it in a photograph. It appeared to be a large three-dimensional sphere with illuminated tentacles stretching out from its middle. Inside were smaller orbs traveling through the appendages and moving toward the center of the object. A few weeks later, he sent me a very interesting e-mail.

He had sent the photo to a gentleman who frequently assists in investigations with high profile members of reality paranormal television programs. He was told he had captured something very rare, the elusive orb catcher. The man who reviewed the photo went on to say, in over three hundred investigations he had never seen or heard of one being captured on video or in a photograph.

So why is 432 Abercorn a paranormal lightning rod? The answer may lie, quite literally, beneath the surface. The house is sitting on top of the largest slave burial ground of the eighteenth century. The remains are still unearthed during development and are undeniably present. The graves are shallow, in mass and overlap. The property is the final resting place for those who toiled under a lifetime of slavery, only to be laid to rest carelessly in makeshift holes.

I am among the scarce few who stand across from the house night after night and receive thousands of emails and photos submitted by hundreds of people over years of time. Being in this privileged position allows me to make an informed conclusion about the home's supernatural credibility. My sincere belief is we will likely go to our own graves never knowing the full story, in large part because it continues to evolve. I am forced

to leave the reader in the same predicament that I find myself...having as many questions as answers.

Out of respect for the owner of the home and the residents who live nearby, please limit any activity around the home to the square. Never, under any circumstances, travel onto the property itself. Besides illegal, those who believe in the strong paranormal presence of the location, say it could be quite dangerous.

Beth Dolgner runs a blog which includes a great section on 432 Abercorn at bethdolgner.com

Chris Allen pointed out a strange, fun fact about the home...its city ID number. Every property in Chatham County has a property record card with a 5 digit number assigned it. 432 Abercorn's number? 66666.

SECTION FOUR ✤ *The Hag*

In May of 2012, BASE productions, the studio responsible for the new Syfy show *Paranormal Highway* asked me to speak on the subject of *Hags*. They wanted to send a crew from Los Angeles to Savannah if I could appear on the episode and provide a few witnesses. I've been asked to do interviews and story development on paranormal subject matter for years...but never on the *Hag*. This interest confirmed two things: awareness of this particular phenomena is growing, and Savannah is considered the heart of Hag country. So if you plan on dabbling in the paranormal when coming here, pay close attention to this section.

The most relatable story we tell on our tour is that of the Hag. Almost without exception, in a crowd of thirty, there will be at least one person who contacts me after the tour, divulging they or someone they know has had an encounter.

Hags are dark inhabitants from parts unknown. They go by other deviant titles you may be more familiar with such as *Shadow People*, *Shadow Skin*, *Plat-Eye*, *Shape Shifters* and *Slip Skins* to name a few.

I have studied the subject intensely since my own encounter (reference the story in this book: And Then She Melted). I chill as I look back and realize many of my freshman investigations were actually locations experiencing Hag phenomena, rather than some garden variety haunting. I shudder in hindsight at my ignorance and the bad advice I gave.

Since then, I've cringed as websites like *Wikipedia* have lumped Hag phenomena in with *sleep paralysis* simply because they share only three of more than two dozen known symptoms. Nearly all Savannah tour guides and operators treat the subject with respect but occasionally I've bristled listening to the glib ones...with no firsthand experience, regurgitating information from a half-wit tour operator who was merely cashing in on an industry...or training anyone with a tour guide license for a summer *J-O-B*.

I've shaken my head in concern as I watched well-meaning upstarts with an EMF meter, club t-shirts and a catchy acronym start a "professional" paranormal investigation group, then scratch their head months later when a team member goes off the deep end wondering if they are losing their mind after a brush with this thing.

I've witnessed the aftermath of attacks, bites, cuts and scratches on victims with no pets or animals to account for the marks. I've seen whelps and burn-like wounds in places not conducive with self-mutilation.

I've conducted investigations in "Hag houses" and have a friend who will no longer speak to me because I took him to a home where he experienced the phenomena. He poked his head into an empty attic to investigate claw-like scratching sounds we were picking up and had his teeth kicked in by a full-formed shadow. He was a non-believing, master's level, electrical engineer. He asked to go on the investigation so he could play with the gadgetry. He is now a fully converted ex-friend who blames me for not shaking him by the shoulders and saying...*Hags are real.*

I've interviewed socially functional, professionally successful, well-adjusted members of the community literally questioning their sanity... terrified because they were being attacked. I've watched spouses cry and worry the thing they saw assaulting their loved one, would someday day kill them.

I've interviewed Father Gary Thomas, Vatican trained and known as "America's Top Exorcist". A movie, *The Rite*, was released detailing his experiences. We discussed the matter in all seriousness and he was able to relate to the phenomena.

The first documented occurrence I've found is in ancient China roughly five thousand years ago, around the same time as the *I Ching,* the ancient Chinese oracle. The reference to the *"pressing ghost"* wasn't found on papyrus or a cave wall; it was found etched in *bone.* How impactful would an event need to be for you to etch the experience in bone? Four thousand years ago the Mongolians called this thing, *"The Dark Presser".* The literal application would be shadows come to life. Think about that... shadows...come to *life.*

It is possible that even Christ spoke of these things. He encountered certain dark spirits he did not cast out in the usual way, by invoking the name of God as a rebuke. When confronting this type of energy Jesus advises, *"But this kind does not leave except by prayer and fasting."* Matthew 17:2.

So please, consider this your literary 'shake'. *Hags are real.*

The Hag encompasses an entire section because it is the haunted, moonlit bridge between the mysterious and mystical Conjurers section of this book and the straightforward, structured world of the Colonial section. The Hag permeates both worlds in countless stories. It can be said: *The Hag knows no bounds.*

In all references, it seems to operate as a psychic vampire of sorts. It feeds off the unhappiness of people, using negative spiritual energy to prolong manifestation on this plane.

It commonly preys on women, primarily those who have struggled with chronic depression or deep sadness most of their lives. It also seems to favor women with heightened psychic openness or who have had a major traumatic event, such as a miscarriage, or the death of a young child. Post-partum has been perceived as a key doorway as well.

The best reason I've heard put forth as to why it targets women, comes courtesy of a sufferer and psychically gifted woman. She concludes, since women are generally more psychically open than men, the Hag is a tradeoff. Receiving psychic and spiritual impressions at a greater rate and frequency, means they also broadcast at a greater rate and frequency. If your transmission is negative in nature…you can become the safe harbor, a food source, an oasis for the thing.

After many studies, investigations and interviews on the subject, I have some of my own theories. Take them for what you will. Chief among them is the progression of the attacks.

The first thing that happens is the brain (some might say *soul)* discerns a presence. Have you ever heard the anecdote of someone dreaming they were eating a giant marshmallow and when they woke up their pillow was gone? It's a base way of saying; the brain takes things that are literal and communicates them through imagery. I once dreamt I was in my car with blinding headlights headed toward me. I woke with the morning sun coming through the window, hitting me dead in the eyes. The brain is a wild place, man.

For Hag sufferers, the brain causes the person to dream but contrary to the above examples, the details are incoherent. They wake with a sense of dread or impending doom. An anxiety attack is common. Within moments, they see the 8-10 foot shadow standing ominously at the end of the bed or slowly moving across the room.

"Feeling hate coming from unseen eyes" is customarily mentioned and occasionally a foul smells fill the nostrils (rotten meat, sulfur). It is darker than the dark surrounding it. No matter how black the room, its form can be traced against the night. Most people report putting their head under the covers and either laying in fear, or silently praying. I've yet to meet anyone who had the courage to go after it. I'm not mocking them; I didn't go after it either. Everyone has a game plan until they get hit.

This is usually as far as it goes. However, a society that lends itself to depression and unhappiness all but assures some will progress further. Chronic sufferers will, at some point, report physical contact with the dark form. This is likely the phenomena the Mongolians and Turks were communicating with the name, *"Dark Presser."* Upon waking, the person may hear a humming, hissing or buzzing in the ear. In a few cases, a strange and unintelligible dialect could be heard coming from the whispering frequency.

Most people say they wake with a crushing black form on their chest. In the low country, it is referred to as, *"Riding the Hag"* or *"Hag Ridden"*. The person will complain of feeling smothered, strangled or held down. In a few reports, people sleeping in the nude said it felt like raw meat was pressed against them. Another said the breath smelled like *"burped sulfur"*.

A very few experience horrific physical and psychic attacks indefinitely. Those who experience encounters of this magnitude are usually in for a long, rough road, although it is exceptionally rare.

For me, the strangest part of the phenomena is those targeted are unable to find relief through traditional spiritual methods. They are said to be resistant even to exorcism. The reason being, unlike demons, Hags don't *possess*; they *oppress*. Rites of exorcism don't work because the problem is not *in* the individual, but rather *on* them.

I have spoken with people who have moved several times over the years, sometimes specifically in an attempt to escape the attacks...to no avail. When I discussed this with a priest, I was shocked to hear him say, "Well, yes, I have heard of this and it seems to be the one thing that **can** follow you home." I don't buckle easy, but that caused me to rethink where and how I would conduct investigations going forward, especially in Savannah.

INFESTATION ❧

There are books, blogs and armchair experts that will diagram how to conduct paranormal investigations, some of which are quite useful. In lieu of that large repository of information, I will refrain and instead outline how to conduct investigations in a location experiencing Hag phenomenon or as a woman who spoke with me in 2009 called it, an *infestation*.

During preliminary research, we will typically investigate the reputation of anyone claiming a haunting. You might be amazed at what camera-hungry people are willing to say to get a reputable group into their homes. We are licensed, bonded and insured. We require liability waivers signed by the verified owner of any property we investigate. If necessary, we conduct background checks on the people involved and we charge for all expenses. Say what you will but investigating a Hag infestation is not a viable way to make a living. In addition to the large amount of risk involved, we also use about $30,000 worth of equipment and spend hundreds of hours researching, investigating the location, and processing the results. A word of warning, remain extremely suspect of the skills and motivations of any *pro bono* investigation group.

Hag activity is primarily isolated to the sufferer as opposed to the structure. This is the reason moving usually proves to be a futile effort. If the home is showing signs of phenomenon however, it will frequently be in the bedroom of the sufferer and most often take the form of a stationery cold spot. If we are to believe popular paranormal theories, manifested entities are consuming energy from the space around them in order to remain on an earthly plane and this is the reason cold spots typically exist in haunted properties. In Hag cases, the cold spot is usually above the bed and at least ten degrees colder than the average temperature of the room. It gives the impression of dark, oppressive clouds roosting above the sleeping victim. Occasionally, long-time sufferers have switched rooms or started sleeping on the couch, only to find the cold spot move with them shortly afterward. It is wise to be specific as to the location of the bedroom and the actual sleeping quarters...they may not necessarily be the same.

Contrary to ordinary hauntings, when we ask the residents to leave the property or stay in the background, in a Hag infestation the sufferer takes center stage. Cameras and monitoring equipment are set up, usually in the bedroom or other area where the victim spends personal time. It is often necessary to monitor the person while they sleep, specifically focusing on the area around the victim. We prefer to observe the activity from a different part of the home, ideally a room located on the other end of the house.

Some of the equipment we use is standard for most any paranormal investigation, but infestations require certain complex luxury items. The first essential is a great, not good, thermal imager, and ideally more than one. Currently we use the Flir i7. With price tags in the thousands, they are indeed expensive but this type of equipment separates the amateur from the professional researcher in terms of capability during an investigation. These devices are mandatory for accurate temperature readings and to photo-capture anomalies.

Another very useful piece of equipment is an air ion counter. Proper use of this device would be tedious if not impossible for a beginner, but the general purpose is to measure the electro*static*, rather than the electro*magnetic*, field of an area. The theory at work here is, as energy or matter moves through the air, it encounters molecules and this inherently cause static due to friction. This agitation results in additional ions. It has taken years to efficiently integrate the counter into investigations and I could write a thesis on interpreting the readings correctly. For the purpose of overview, suffice it to say, we have captured incredible anomalies in photographs using air ion counters when EMF detectors had proved useless.

One piece of equipment we use may be foreign to even seasoned investigators, the grid light. It is a modified improvement over the standard green dot device. If you aren't familiar with either, the green dot device is a simple tripod-mounted pointer that projects onto walls. Any entities, orbs or otherworldly shadows would be discerned by passing thru the speckled pattern. Videotaping the room where these dots are projected allows you to go back and actually trace the shape of the anomaly. Using a grid system is superior for obvious reasons. It delivers an uninterrupted, interlocking pattern onto surfaces like walls and ceilings and provides a greater comprehensive coverage. This combination allows a much more accurate depiction of the phenomena. Observing a humanoid shadow pass thru a grid system in a closed room full of seated observers is quite a sight.

Video footage of this is not posted due to the high impact of watching it, coupled with the monetary motivations we have as a ghost tour company. We have always felt it would be beyond believable for the casual observer; it is easy to fake and we don't take people on Hag investigations anyway. Our conclusion has ultimately been it would not be worth the controversy and division it would surely cause.

case STUDIES ➤

JILL

"After my divorce, my grandparents owned several houses in the town I grew up in and invited me to move into a quaint farmhouse that sat in the southeast corner of nearly 200 acres. The land had been in our family for almost one hundred years. I was reluctant, but at the time I didn't have a job and the home I shared with my husband had recently sold. I was living off of my share of the money while I searched for a job and tried to figure out my options.

The house was small but functional. I was looking forward to some quiet time and at first, my stay was uneventful. That didn't last very long. I began waking up in the middle of the night with an extreme coldness coming from the end of my bed. I would see a black form standing there at the foot of it. It would disappear almost as soon as I saw it. This went on for a few weeks and even though it was extremely unsettling, I had chalked it up to my own imagination...strange shadows being cast by the trees and moonlight. It wasn't until I was attacked that I knew it had been real all along.

I woke up and I was being strangled. I tried to move but my body wouldn't work. It was just blackness on top of me. I remember feeling pressure against my ear and a hissing sound pushed through it like it was trying to speak, but I couldn't understand what it was trying to say. I heard something like a baby crying, then the sound of laughing. I felt sick. I had a miscarriage seven months before this happened and was still severely depressed. The accompanying guilt was the death nail in my marriage. The memory of losing my child is still with me and at the time, I felt I was such a failure there was no hope of ever becoming a mother or being a wife. I was convinced this thing knew all of that. It was able to see the most painful parts of me and was mocking it. It wanted me to be afraid. It was feeding on it. I remember there was a very offensive odor in the room but I can't remember what it was or what to even compare it to (spoiled meat, maybe.) There was too much going on. I was completely subjected to the experience. I just kept thinking...I'm going to die.

As I fought to regain control of my body and mind, I realized I was being overtaken. My body was frozen. My mind was under attack and my fight was slipping away. At some point my will to survive rose up for a second and in that moment, I screamed No! Finally, the thing let go of me. I felt the grip slide down my body. Once it got to my feet, it grabbed my ankles and pulled me down the mattress. I was now half on the bed and the tips of my toes were touching the floor. It tried to mount me again, so I screamed, Get off me! Get out of here! It let go of me slowly and coolly. It faded away, almost blending with the blackness of the dark. I watched it become like smoke and turn into something slim, almost snakelike. It then compressed and became about the width of a sheet of paper. I watched, crying, as it slowly disappeared through the corner of my room where wall and ceiling meet.

I barely had the strength to get off the bed. I was locked in place by fear but it was scarier to stay put than run into the night and the safety of my car. I sat with my knees against my chest, my back firmly against the headboard. I knew my keys were on the table by the front door. I breathed heavily trying to muster the nerve to move. I took one last heavy breath and leaped off the bed. I shot through the living room and grabbed my keys as I passed by the table. I pushed the front door open and tore out the small nail holding the lock on the old screen door. I never looked back. I climbed into my car hitting my head as I slid behind the driver's seat. My foot was trembling on the gas pedal all the way to my grandparents' house, several miles away, where I arrived still in pajamas.

I pounded on the door and the porch light came on. They threw open the door and I fell into my grandmothers arms and cried. Finally, I said I had been attacked. My grandfather asked if I knew who it was and I told him it wasn't a man. My grandfather looked stunned. I saw him walk out the door with his pistol with my grandmother nervously telling him to be careful. While he was gone, I told the story as my grandmother listened. My grandfather called my two brothers and they rode to the house convinced it was an intruder. My fear convinced them something real happened, but they were too shocked to consider the possibility it was otherworldly.

The house was checked but nothing was found amiss. There was no sign of forced entry or robbery. When my grandmother looked at my neck, she saw red whelps that looked like an allergic reaction but nothing that resembled hand prints. My grandfather and brothers, now back, stood in the kitchen listening to the story in full detail. My grandfather looked bothered and said there was nothing in the house, but he had noticed one strange thing. The air at the end of that bed was as cold as ice. It had been apparent as soon as he walked in the room.

I didn't stay in the house after that night. I moved in with my mother. A family ended up renting the house and while they have remarked about the cold spot, nothing unusual has happened. I still go to bed afraid it was me and not the house this thing was haunting. I always think one night I'll wake up and it will be back."

JESSICA

"It has only happened once. I woke up terrified. I didn't know what was happening. It was like my body was having an experience apart from me. I was trembling. I felt a heaviness covering me. It was as if Hope itself was being driven out of me and this covering of depression was taking its place. I could actually *feel* it watching me from the end of my bed. My ceilings are 10 feet tall and what would have been its head was nearly touching it. My room was completely dark but I could see this form against the blackness. It was darker than dark.

It wasn't elongated like a shadow being cast. It was erect and uniform. I couldn't see any features but I could sense the hate it had for me. I remember feeling like a child and believing the quilt I was under could save me. I tried to pretend like I didn't see it but as I slid under the covers I knew it was staring at me through the sheets. I started to pray. I don't know for how long. I just did it softly and quietly until I stopped shaking. I slowly peeked out from under the covers and I didn't see the shape against the darkness anymore. I have never been so afraid and I still don't know what kept me calm. A voice in my heart just kept saying do not get off the bed."

CHARLES

"Charles doesn't like to discuss it but I can tell when it's happened to him. He is completely drained and unhappy for days. I've only seen it once but I saw enough to know it is real. He isn't dreaming or crazy. I woke up beside him and had this terrible fear running through me. I looked over at Charles; he was wide-eyed and trying to scream but couldn't move. I could see his body trying to break free. I screamed his name and saw a very large shadow come out of him or off him…I'm not sure which, but it moved faster than anything I have ever seen. It spilled off the mattress and went under the bed. It was hissing like a cat, but deeper. We were holding each other as it kicked us through the mattress and the force of the blows broke us apart. I screamed and grabbed Charles. And then it was just gone. I started sobbing and once we calmed down, he told me how it all started.

He and his mother were born in Haiti. He said they had been following him since he was six years old. His mother had been a conjurer and they lived in Haiti until he was seven. I don't remember exactly what she practiced, but I know it involved allowing spirits to control her body.

She used to sip wine and smoke cigars while the spirits were in her. She told Charles the spirits would use her body to enjoy certain things they liked and in return, they would grant her favor. Rum was their favorite. Sometimes, a certain spirit would take control of her and Charles would hear her in the next room, playing with a baby rattle and laughing like a child. The shadow started following him after this particular spirit began showing up more often.

He would wake in the middle of the night with the sheets being pulled from beneath the bed and voices would start talking to him. They wanted him to get under the bed. Sometimes he would hear a gravelly voice saying "plaaay", "plaaay". He would stand on the bed and scream. His mother would run in and encourage him to get off the bed but he was convinced it would pull him under and strangle him to death. She put brooms at his door and salt around his bed. He said it actually helped. I'm scared one day they are going to kill him."

the GOOD FIGHT ✦

Most Hag sufferers want to know if and how to get rid of them. I don't have an easy answer. Years of study have caused me to reach only a few conclusions. The primary one, people can find a way to become an inhospitable host and gain some measure of relief by regaining their joy. I usually shy away from New Age buzz phrases, but people who *change their frequency* seem to genuinely find freedom from this mysterious phenomenon. I've also noticed, those who have been opening themselves up psychically to any form of spiritual experimentation seem to find relief when they become more discriminating in their practices. Doing so will be specific to the sufferer, so it really does come down to working out your own salvation. I have also seen a great deal of relief when a 'cleansing' is performed on the home or location where the disturbance is occurring. I have witnessed this ceremony carried out with success by members of Catholic and Episcopal clergy, Conjurers, and New Age practitioners. I am not suggesting these are the only viable avenues, they are merely the remedies I have seen produce positive results.

In fact, everything considered, the denominational affiliation of the acting agent battling the Hag may differ, but the principle seems to be the same. At its core, it is a struggle between that which is customarily regarded as *good* …and that, which is *evil*.

BIBLIOGRAPHY ❧

"Hag." *Wikipedia, The Free Encyclopedia*. Wikipedia, The Free Encyclopedia, 9 May. 2012. Web. 19 May. 2012.

"Alice Riley - Savannah, Georgia Ghosts." *Alice Riley - Savannah, Georgia Ghosts*. Web. Apr.-May 2012. <http://savannahghostpost.com/Alice.aspx>.

"Historic Wright Square." *Wright Square*. Web. Apr.-May 2012. <http://www.visit-historic-savannah.com/wrightsquare.html>.

"Saved by the Bell." *Saved by the Bell*. Web. Mar.-Apr. 2012. <http://www.phrases.org.uk/meanings/saved-by-the-bell.html>.

"Weird & Wonderful Patents - Coffin with Escape Hatch." *Weird & Wonderful Patents - Coffin with Escape Hatch*. Web. Apr.-May 2012. <http://www.bpmlegal.com/wcoffin.html>.

"Georgia." *Georgia*. Web. Mar.-Apr. 2012. <http://earthquake.usgs.gov/earthquakes/states/georgia/history.php>.

"The Difference Between -Shade-and-Shadow/." *The Difference Between-Shade-and-Shadow*. Web. Apr.-May 2012. <http://www.dailywritingtips.com/the-difference-between-shade-and-shadow/>.

"Kathryn Tucker Windham." *Wikipedia.* Wikimedia Foundation, 05 Oct. 2012. Web. Apr.-May 2012. <http://en.wikipedia.org/wiki/Kathryn_Tucker_Windham>.

"True Hauntings of America: Haunts of the 17 Hundred 90 Inn and Tavern." *True Hauntings of America: Haunts of the 17 Hundred 90 Inn and Tavern.* Web. Apr.-May 2012. <http://hauntsofamerica.blogspot.com/2011/03/haunts-of-17-hundred-90-inn-and-tavern.html>.

"Georgia History Timeline / Chronology 1820." *Georgia History Timeline / Chronology 1820.* Web. Apr.-May 2012. <http://ourgeorgiahistory.com/year/1820>.

"Cemetery Guide." *Cemetery Guide.* Web. Apr.-May 2012. <http://www.savannahga.gov/cityweb/cemeteriesweb.nsf/6f01764198462d668525703b006b1481/e01a90e6d51e7dfd85257035006620ca?OpenDocument>.

"Savannah Specters." *: Exorcism at The Hampton Lillibridge House.* Web. Apr.-May 2012. <http://savannahspecters.blogspot.com/2009/02/exorcism-at-hampton-lillibridge-house.html>.

"Haunted Crime Scenes: Savannah's 'Most Haunted' House." *Haunted Crime Scenes: Hampton-Lillibridge Is Savannah's Most Haunted House â Savannah's 'Most Haunted' House â Crime Library on TruTV.com.* Web. Apr.-May 2012. <http://www.trutv.com/library/crime/notorious_murders/classics/hampton-lillibridge/1_index.html>.

"Exorcisms within the Anglican/Episcopal Church. Do They or Have They Happened in Recent Memory? - Anglicans & Episcopalians - Beliefnet Community." *Exorcisms within the Anglican/Episcopal Church. Do They - or Have They - Happened in Recent Memory? - Anglicans & Episcopalians - Beliefnet Community.* Web. Mar.-Apr. 2012. <http://community.beliefnet.com/go/thread/view/44071/21945137/Exorcisms_within_the_AnglicanEpiscopal_Church.__Do_they_-_or_have_they_-_happened_in_recent_memory>.

Kanade, Shrinivas. "Grim Reaper Origin And History." *Buzzle.com.* Buzzle.com, 02 Jan. 2012. Web. 11 Apr. 2012. <http://www.buzzle.com/ articles/grim-reaper-origin-and-history.html>.

"The Crossroads in Hoodoo Magic and The Ritual of Selling Yourself to the Devil." TheCrossroads. Web. Mar.- Apr. 2012. <http://www.lucky-mojo.com/crossroads.html>.

"About Us - Oyotunji.org." *Oyotunji.org.* Web. Spring 2012. <http:// www.oyotunji.org/about-us.html>.

Caskey, James. *Haunted Savannah: The Official Guidebook to Savannah Haunted History Tour Conducted by Cobblestone Tours, Inc.* Savannah, GA: Bonaventture, 2005: 105

Stevens, John R. *Voodoo: Strange Fascinating Tales and Lore.* New York: Fall River, 2010. Print.
Puckett, Newbell Niles. *Folk Beliefs of the Southern Negro,.* Chapel Hill: University of North Carolina, 1926. Print.

Drums and Shadows; Survival Studies among the Georgia Coastal Negroes. Athens: University of Georgia, 1940. Print.

Caskey, James. *Haunted Savannah: The Official Guidebook to Savannah Haunted History Tour Conducted by Cobblestone Tours, Inc.* Savannah, GA: Bonaventture, 2005: 37

the WORLD *of* BLUE ORB ✦

GHOST TOURS

Uncensored Zombie Tour with Tobias McGriff
This tour is truly an adult pleasure. It is for ages 18 and older and is led by Blue Orb Founder, Tobias McGriff. Advance booking is recommended and reservations are required.

City of the Dead
This is a creepy, in-depth tour good for all ages, however, parental discretion is advised due to mature themes. Guide varies. Reservations required.

CEMETERY TOURS

Tour Bonaventure
This is a fully guided historical journey through one of America's most beautiful Victorian cemeteries. Photo opportunities are plentiful and include round trip transportation from downtown Savannah in climate controlled shuttles. Space is limited and reservations are required.

PODCAST
Savannah Shadows (formerly known as *Savannah Paranormal*)-

Broadcasts from America's most haunted city and attracts over 25,000 listeners, *Savannah Shadows* is hosted by Tobias McGriff and includes guest co-hosts and interviews with well-known paranormal icons such as Amityville survivor Christopher Lutz and Vatican trained exorcist Father Gary Thomas. iTunes keywords: *Savannah Shadows*.

FILM

Hag
Documentary
Release Date: 2013
Studio: Round1Productions
Written, Directed and Produced by Tobias McGriff

EBOOK

Hag - Late 2012

WEBSITES

blueorbtours.com
savannahshadows.com
tourbonaventure.com

SOCIAL NETWORKS

Keywords: Blue Orb Tours

RECOMMENDATIONS ✦

RESTAURANTS

B. Matthews Eatery
Conveniently located on Bay Street, this is a go-to spot for breakfast and brunch (Saturday and Sunday). A great wait staff and laid-back atmosphere compliment the Bay Street Scramble, and the contradictory but delicious French toast made with Portuguese sweet bread.
Information: *bmatthewseatery.com*

Subdogs Hot Doggery
Calories consumed on vacation don't count, so rack them up at this gourmet hot dog heaven. They are new to Savannah and based on what I've tasted so far, they are here to stay. The Super Brah is my latest addiction, and is topped with smoked pulled pork, southern slaw, butter pickles and 7 brothers mustard.
Information: *subdogshotdoggery.com*

Corleone's Trattoria
Besides containing a hidden paranormal gem courtesy of the haunted basement, this is Italian comfort food at its best. Rob is the evil genius who put Corleone's back on the culinary map. Hint: Tomato Bisque. You won't be sorry.
Information: *corleones.tv*

GHOST TOURS

6th Sense World

Headed by Angela Lynn, *6th Sense World* is not afraid to try new things and has a wide variety of offerings. It's one of the original walking ghost tour companies and they have expanded to offer guided paranormal investigations as well. Tour spots go quickly and attract large crowds. Advanced booking is recommended.
Information: *6thsenseworld.com*

Haunted Savannah Tours

This is a new tour company spearheaded by ambitious upstart, Chris Allen. Ordinarily I don't recommend a new company, but I've actually taken this tour and I know Chris to be a competent researcher. The guest feedback I've gotten in the six months he has been in business has been impressive. Chris goes the extra mile and is passionate about pleasing his guests. I recommend him if you enjoy a smaller crowd and a less formal tour.
Information: *hauntedsavannahtours.com*

Hearse Tours

Creepy, cheesy and cheap are the words I hear most often about Hearse Tours. And they are meant in the best possible way. The tours are family friendly, affordable and offer the chance to tour Savannah in retired, modified hearses with guides like "Peg Leg Ron" and "Lunatic Laura". If walking isn't your thing, then *Hearse Tours* is the best way to go.
Information: *hearseghosttours.com*

PUB CRAWLS

Cobblestone Tours

Cobblestone offers a walking ghost and history tour but I think all would agree they are best known for the pub-crawl. James Caskey is the founder and the author of *Haunted Savannah*. He is regarded as one of

the best researchers of Savannah history and he imparts that knowledge to his guides. The pub crawl is two hours of extremely affordable fun.
Information: *ghostsavannah.com*

Tara Tours
Tara Ryan is one of the few tour operators who are not only a Savannah native, but a multi-generational one. Her family owned the famed Kehoe House and she is hip to most everything spooky that has happened here. Her *Boos and Brews* tour is very popular and I also recommend her for girl scouts and large groups.
Information: *taratourssavannah.com*

Creepy Crawl
Greg Profitt is the New England mastermind behind this popular pub-crawl. His loud voice, raucous ghost stories and sarcastic comments to other tour guides (me) as he passes by, will keep you entertained for hours.
Information: *savannahtours.com*

HISTORY TOURS

Explore Savannah
Bobby Davis has daytime touring down to a science. He is a *Trip Advisor* legend and I've never heard a cross word about his tour. If you want a custom fit daytime walking tour, this is the guy.
Information: *exploresavannah.com*

Savannah Dan
You can't miss Dan in his seersucker suit and bowtie. This is another tour I never hesitate to recommend to anyone looking for a daytime history tour.
Information: *savannahdan.com*

Savannah Belle
Michelle Freenor has a wide range of experience conducting tours

in Savannah. She is the one to call if you like walking history tours, smaller crowds, and personal service. She might even throw in a ghost story or two.
Information: *savannahbelletours.com*

Savannah River Street Pirates
The pirate ship *Renegade* boards from River Street and is my pick for "Most Original Tour" in 2012. It is long overdue and offers guests the chance to participate in a live pirate show complete with water cannons.
Information: *savannahriverstreetpirates.com*

Bonaventure Cemetery Tours
6th Sense World offers a walking tour of *Bonaventure Cemetery* and is one of the first companies to do so. It is consistently rated as one of the best and I hear nothing but good things.
Information: *bonaventurecemeterytours.com*

PSYCHIC SERVICES

Kelly Spurlock
Kelly is currently the only psychic in Savannah I am willing to recommend. She hails from West Virginia, but she has found her spiritual home in Savannah. She is available by phone and in-person and she will come to you for readings.
Information: *facebook.com/SavannahPsychic*

ACKNOWLEDGEMENTS ✦

The effort that has produced this quality, keepsake reference for all of the strangeness that is Savannah was made possible by the following contributors:

Book Design by Rebecca Lysen
Photography by Beau Kester
Editing by Ashley Shy
Original Musical Score by Richard Leo Johnson

SPECIAL THANKS:
The people of Oyotunji
Chasity Jordan
Mindy Shea
James Caskey
The staff of the Savannah Visitor's Center
The hotels and inns that trust their guests to Blue Orb Tours
Patrick Godley for allowing us to film at the 17hundred90 Inn & Restaurant
Rob and the Corleone's Trattoria staff
Terence McKenna
Kathryn Tucker Windham
Mark Eggers
Bradley Dilling

ABOUT *the* AUTHOR ❧

Tobias McGriff is the author of *Savannah Shadows: Tales from the Midnight Zombie Tour* and host of *Savannah Paranormal* on WTKS 1290 every Saturday from 11 p.m. until Midnight EST. *Savannah Paranormal* can also be heard anytime on podcast (iTunes keywords: *Savannah Paranormal*). Tobias has interviewed such guests as Amityville survivor Christopher Lutz and Vatican trained exorcist, Father Gary Thomas, featured in *The Rite*.

Tobias is a professional member of the Rhine Research Center and is widely regarded as an expert on supernatural phenomena and the haunted history of the southern United States. He has also done story development for multiple paranormal reality programs and has been featured on the *Syfy* channel's *Paranormal Highway* and many popular regional programs such as *New Day Cleveland*.

In 2010, he unveiled *Blue Orb Tours,* a specialty walking tour company that was named *The Destination Guides* "Best Savannah Ghost Tour 2011".

Publicist: Sara Sgarlat (434) 245-2272 or sgarlatpublicity@comcast.net.